IS THAT YOUR

HAND

IN MY

POCKET?

IS THAT YOUR
HAND
IN MY
POCKET?

THE SALES PROFESSIONAL'S GUIDE
TO NEGOTIATING

RON LAMBERT & TOM PARKER

NELSON BUSINESS
A Division of Thomas Nelson Publishers
Since 1798

www.thomasnelson.com

Published in Nashville, Tennessee, by Thomas Nelson, Inc.

Nelson Books titles may be purchased in bulk for educational, business, fundraising, or sales promotional use. For information, please e-mail SpecialMarkets@ThomasNelson.com.

Library of Congress Cataloging-in-Publication Data

Lambert, Ron, 1946–
    Is that your hand in my pocket? : the sales professional's guide to
negotiating / Ron Lambert and Tom Parker.
        p. cm.
    Includes bibliographical references.
    ISBN 0-7852-1877-7 (hardcover)
    1. Selling. 2. Negotiation in business.   I. Parker, Tom, 1950
June 25–   . II. Title.
    HF5438.25.L353 2006
    658.85—dc22   2005036825

Printed in the United States of America
06 07 08 09 QW 6 5 4 3 2 1

CONTENTS

CONTENTS

ACKNOWLEDGMENTS

A BOOK LIKE THIS IS LESS THE PRODUCT OF SOMEONE'S imagination and more the result of cumulative experience. For this reason, the authors give full credit for whatever insights might be contained in the text to (in this order) our clients, our colleagues (especially John McCormack, Tom Zimmerman, Steve Harris, Dave Burdette, Chris Ayers and Dr. Russ Leonard), our salespeople, the sources listed in the bibliography, and our mentors. A friend, Dave Burns, a retired United States trade negotiator, gets special thanks for sharing some of his experiences for our book.

Special thanks are also due to Debbie and Betsy, our long-suffering spouses who have endured countless birthdays, anniversaries, and PTA meetings alone while the two of us were blasting all over the globe in search of our next big deal.

We also want to thank Susan Caldwell, our operations manager at

Yukon, an Alongside Management company, who has spent countless hours in helping us with this book and the pictures and making sure that we are using proper formats. She has been a great help to both of us.

We would also like to single out Vistage (formerly known as TEC, The Executive Council). Vistage is a worldwide organization of more than ten thousand CEOs of medium-sized companies. The authors have been privileged to work with dozens of Vistage chapters around the country, and the experience has been invaluable to the formation of many concepts presented in the book. Both authors recommend this group without reservation. More information on Vistage is available at www.vistage.com. Some of the stories and examples contained in this book came from our work with Vistage members.

RON LAMBERT

TOM PARKER

INTRODUCTION

RELATIONSHIP SELLING MAY NOT BE AS DEAD AS DISCO (YET), but it needs to get its affairs in order. More and more often, large companies are looking at those cozy vendor relationships that their buyers have, and they are wondering if all that warm, fuzzy, win-win attitude isn't costing them a few points at the bottom line.

Training firms, including our own, have taught salespeople how to build rapport, create equal business standing, and explore alternatives with their clients. The goal of this strategy is to create an atmosphere of trust and mutual respect where the needs of both sides can be explored and, it is hoped, meet with a creative solution that allows both parties to get what they want (or need) out of the negotiation.

When this strategy works, it works great. Here's the rub. It works only if both parties want to play. The problem is this: the global economy has put so much pressure on companies to squeeze costs out of their operations that the purchasing function is increasingly seen as a key profit center.

Several years ago, it became clear to us that there was movement on the buyer side away from the collaborative model and in another direction entirely. In place of relationships and creativity, we got commoditization and reverse auctions. This began with the largest companies and has been gradually morphing its way down the food chain ever since.

Traditional selling skills don't work well in this environment because only one party is playing the game. While the seller is working to build a relationship, the buyer is working just as hard to avoid it. In this scenario, the buyer wins when he can identify multiple sources for the same product or service and then let them beat themselves bloody competing for the order.

This is not to say that relationship selling has gone away or will go away completely (neither will the Bee Gees or Donna Summer, for that matter). There will always be a need for these skills. In today's business climate, however, a salesperson needs to be prepared to play the game either way. This book is aimed at helping salespeople learn to cope successfully and win in this rapidly changing environment. Where collaboration reigns, the skill sets are here to create even more collaboration. Where collaboration is an endangered species, the techniques are here to help salespeople move the other side toward collaboration.

For the last fifteen years, we have taught thousands of salespeople on six different continents how to deal with professional buyers. The skill sets that we will cover in this book have saved those clients almost $2 billion. They will work just as well for you. In addition, these skills will make your negotiations with even the toughest buyers more productive and less stressful. Oh, and as an additional benefit, you'll probably make a lot more money!

Even if you aren't dealing with career purchasing people yet, you owe it to yourself to prepare for the day when you will have to. In the happy event that your industry is not moving in that direction, this book will make you a more effective negotiator inside and outside your company.

This book is dedicated to hardworking sales professionals everywhere.

—RON LAMBERT AND TOM PARKER

CHAPTER 1

WHY BUYERS DON'T WANT YOU TO READ THIS BOOK

As you are reading this sentence, somewhere in the world, a room full of buyers-in-training are going over the tactics and techniques that they will use on you. These techniques are designed to confuse you, to knock you off your carefully put-together game plan, to sap your power, and to pick your pocket.

Pretty scary, huh?

You are a professional salesperson. You've had lots of product training, and you know your stuff. You've had some consultative sales training too, and you know all about the importance of establishing rapport and building relationships with your customers.

Here's something that you might not know. These people couldn't care less. They don't want to be your friends. They don't want to have rapport or a relationship. They want to beat your price down as low as they can, and they don't care if you lose your job or your company goes broke as a result.

They are professional buyers, and they are out to get you.

The world has changed a lot in the last twenty years, and nowhere are those changes more profound than in the age-old equation of "buyer" and "seller." Global trade has brought a lot of benefits to all of us, but one side effect of all this new commerce is ferocious competition.

Big companies swallow up smaller ones, and jobs move all over the globe in search of the most efficient (cheapest) labor markets. Outsourcing has moved beyond sneakers and T-shirts and now includes software, call centers, and even some health care functions. This has created a bare-knuckled business environment that, in many cases, won't allow for the kind of cozy supplier-vendor relationships that served us so well in the past.

Call it the Wal-Mart effect if you want, but the fact is that the beady-eyed professional buyers who used to make up a relatively small percentage of the purchasing function are now a fact of life in more and more industries. If they haven't gotten to yours yet, they are probably coming soon.

Our companies, Alongside Management and Yukon, train salespeople to deal with professional purchasing types. Our typical clients are Fortune 100 companies fielding large, multinational sales forces. These salespeople are often calling on the nine-hundred-pound gorillas of the business world, that is, the Wal-Marts, the Targets, the General Motors, and so on.

Our clients hire us because they have realized that they are sending their salespeople into a gunfight armed with a pocketknife. Buyers have moved much more rapidly to embrace the world economy model, and too often, sellers are still using techniques and strategies from an earlier era.

We find that professional buying organizations are now taking steps to actively thwart the strategies that companies typically use to train their salespeople. For instance, companies will now go to considerable lengths to avoid having their buyers develop personal relationships with vendors. They will institute policies like these:

+ not allowing lunches with vendors
+ not permitting gifts from vendors
+ rotating buyers regularly to prevent friendships from forming with vendors
+ having vendor "shoot-outs" with competing companies assembled in a room or a hallway to bid on a piece of business
+ holding online reverse auctions with no sales input

In addition, buyers are taught very specific tactics to use on vendors. These tactics can be devastatingly effective if the salesperson isn't trained in the appropriate countertactics. That's where we come in. We specialize in helping to level the playing field and giving salespeople the tools and the confidence that they need to effectively represent their companies in the marketplace.

This book contains what we've learned from more than forty years of selling, negotiating, managing, teaching, and observing what's going on between buyers and sellers. The skill sets and techniques that we will cover have saved our clients almost $2 billion, and the number is still rising. The best part is that these skill sets will work just as well for you when you set out to buy a car or a piece of furniture as they do when you sit down with your customer to do a big deal.

These techniques are designed to

+ let you sell at higher margins.
+ take pressure off you.
+ counter buyer tactics and strategies.

3

+ make your negotiations smoother and more time-efficient.

+ help you move the other side toward collaboration.

Before we get started, we want to make one final point. It is tempting to think of the battle between buyers and sellers in terms of good and evil. That is, sellers (us) = good, and buyers (them) = evil.

We don't think this is a particularly useful way of thinking. Buyers, after all, have a job to do. If they don't procure products and services at the lowest possible price, they get fired.

It's better to think about this process the way you would a sporting event. Each side has a role to play, and if one side is doing a better job and beating the other, that doesn't make that side bad. That side is just better at playing the game.

We intend not only to give you, our reader, the tools that you need to go out and do a great job for yourself and your company, but also to show you how to have fun while you are at it. As a bonus, these same tools will work just as well when you are negotiating with your boss, your peers, your spouse, and others. You will use these skills for the rest of your life.

When it's your turn to be the buyer, you can turn these same techniques around 180 degrees, and you will be dynamite.

Here are the skill sets that you are going to need:

+ Recognizing negotiation styles—yours and theirs
+ Learning techniques for dealing with the screamers and the bullies
+ Setting a collaborative tone
+ Dealing with buyer tactics
+ Reading nonverbal signals
+ Understanding gender differences in negotiating
+ Learning the art of saving face

+ Planning effectively for a negotiation
+ Choosing the appropriate strategy
+ Using creativity to break deadlocks
+ Understanding power: how to get it and how to keep it
+ Asking *why* questions to uncover buyer motivation
+ Using your team for maximum impact
+ Wrapping up the deal so that it stays closed

As a bonus, we've thrown in a chapter on how to buy a car. We are constantly amazed at the number of successful salespeople who absolutely dread the car buying process. Think about it: this is an opportunity for you to be the customer! We'll show you how to use the techniques and tactics from this book to take the stress out of getting a great deal on your next automotive purchase. In addition, playing the buyer will give you useful insights into the mind of a noncollaborative purchasing person. We can apply this knowledge as we go along.

We've got a lot of ground to cover, so let's get started.

CHAPTER 2

DOES YOUR NEGOTIATING STYLE REALLY MATTER?

ARE NEGOTIATION STYLES REALLY IMPORTANT? READ THIS and decide:

One of our clients in the health care distribution industry worked for more than a year to line up a major agreement with a Fortune 100 company. The CEO of our client's company (let's call him Sam) and his counterpart at the customer company had several formative meetings and had negotiated most of the substantive items in their agreement. A final meeting was set up to go over the terms and move forward on the $250 million deal. When Sam's boss, the chairman of our client's company, heard that this was the final meeting, he invited himself along. Now, before we go any further, you need to know that Sam is a collaborative negotiator and a really nice guy. His chairman (we'll call him Mr. Big) is neither. He is a hard-charging, tough negotiator and has the personality of Genghis Khan. Even though the deal was all but signed, the outcome of that face-to-face meeting was a phone call from the customer the next day to Sam explaining that as long as Mr. Big owned Sam's company, there would never be an agreement between the two companies, ever!

So does style matter? You bet it does. Ask Sam about the $250 million deal that got away.

Each of us has a natural negotiating style. This style is the result of several factors: our upbringing, education, role models, what has worked for us in the past, and more. Although there is no right or wrong style, there are times when using an inappropriate style can get you in a lot of trouble.

For example, the style that you use to negotiate an internal matter with a colleague is probably (we hope) not the same style that you would use when buying a car.

Good negotiators and good salespeople are aware of their natural styles, and they can recognize the styles that others are using with them. They are able to modify their styles according to the situation. In this chapter, we'll show you how and when to do that.

First a word of clarification: negotiating styles are different from behavioral types. Most of us have been through the four styles model (analytical/driver/expressive/amiable) at some point in our careers. These behavioral types are related to but different from negotiating styles. These differences will become clear as we move through the chapter.

One big difference between behavioral types and negotiating styles is that while behavioral types are fairly constant (on the customer side), good negotiators will move from style to style depending on the context of the negotiation. Recognizing when and how to use the different styles can quite often mean the difference between getting the order and getting pulverized at the negotiating table.

Your negotiating style is created by combining the relative importance of the two factors that are always present in every negotiation process:

1. Concern for the people in the negotiation. Your negotiation style may change based on how much you value the relationship and how long you want the relationship to last.
2. The issue being negotiated, such as a supplier's price or service. This is sometimes referred to as the substance of the negotiation.

We refer to this as the PI (People/Issues) Factor. Some blend of these factors produce the four negotiating styles: conquer, collaborate, concede, and compromise.

Based on your background, your negotiating style will fall somewhere on the PI grid depicted here. Most people have a pretty good idea of where to put themselves.

THE PI (PEOPLE/ISSUES) FACTOR

HIGH ↑	**C-1** **CONQUER** PI FACTOR=HIGH FOCUS ON ISSUES/LOW FOCUS ON PEOPLE	**C-2** **COLLABORATE** PI FACTOR=HIGH FOCUS ON ISSUES/HIGH FOCUS ON PEOPLE
CONCERN FOR ISSUES	**C-3** **CONCEDE** PI FACTOR=LOW FOCUS ON ISSUES/HIGH FOCUS ON PEOPLE	**C-4** **COMPROMISE** PI FACTOR=LOW FOCUS ON ISSUES/LOW FOCUS ON PEOPLE

LOW ——————— CONCERN FOR PEOPLE ———————→ HIGH

9

> ➤ PROFESSIONAL NEGOTIATING TIP
>
> Effective salespeople are aware of their styles and recognize the style of the other party. They then make a conscious decision to use the style most appropriate to the occasion.

You can see from the model that your style is determined by the relative importance that you assign each of the two elements of the negotiation, the issues and the people. Remember, there is no one right or wrong style for all occasions. Rather, there is a time and a place for each style to be effective. There are also times when each of them will get you into trouble.

We will now discuss each of the four styles—their strengths and weaknesses, when to use them, and when the use of an inappropriate style might get you into trouble.

C1: Conquer

Based on the model, it is easy to see why we call this style conquer. We all have to work with C1's. (Some of you are C1's!) It is a very common style in our culture. C1's care about the issues, and they want to win. Our favorite description of this style is "two dogs/one bone." They aren't particularly interested in how the other party feels, and they don't put a lot of value on relationships. Sound familiar?

People adopt this style for various reasons. Sometimes they've learned this style from their role models. Some people use it defensively. That is, they feel that others might take advantage of them if they aren't aggressive. At any rate, it is a common style among professional buyers, and we need to know how to deal with it.

Let's look at situations in which this style is effective and some in which it isn't.

C1 is effective when

+ it's a one-time deal and you'll never see the other party again.
+ you have a dominant market position and the other party has no choice but to deal with you (be careful here, because the other party will probably hate you and constantly look for another source).
+ you can't/won't negotiate on this particular point (i.e., a moral issue, a legal issue, a safety situation, a company policy, etc.).
+ the other party is using C1.

Think about it. If they are coming at you in a strong conquer mode, what's going to happen if you try to collaborate, concede, or compromise? You are going to get creamed.

In these situations, it is often very effective to go to C1. You need to stand up to the other person in order to show him that you aren't going to roll over. Once he realizes that this style isn't going to work, he will, quite often, move to another style that will be easier to work with. Many C1's have C4 (compromise) as their backup style.

C1 is not the best style for

+ internal negotiations with peers, subordinates, or superiors.
+ outside negotiations with important long-term subcontractors and clients.
+ differences of opinion with a spouse or significant other.

Negotiation tips for dealing with C1's include the following:

+ Move quickly to establish equal business standing (see Chapter 4).

+ Stand firm, show them that you can't be bullied or bluffed, and they are likely to default into a style that you can deal with more effectively.

+ Find a way to let them think that they have won something for themselves or their company.

Negotiation tips for you if you are a C1 include the following:

+ Be aware of your tendency to ignore people's feelings.

+ Where appropriate, take the time to look for the win-win as opposed to win-lose.

> PROFESSIONAL NEGOTIATING TIP

If C1 is your style, don't win the battle and lose the war where ongoing relationships are important.

C2: Collaborate

This style is great for most business negotiations. The model shows that C2's place a lot of emphasis on the issues and the people side of the equation. In order to make this style work, C2's need to find a way to get what they want and make the other party feel good about the deal. This involves both parties working together to come up with a win-win solution. To make this happen, both sides have to share information and ideas and look for a creative solution.

Sounds great, doesn't it? We'd like all of our negotiations to be this way. The problem is, collaboration is effective only if both parties see the benefit and work together. If only one party is collaborating and the other is in a conquer mode, the results can be ugly. That is why it is critical for good negotiators and salespeople to be able to recognize styles.

C2 is a great style for

+ internal negotiations.
+ important supplier and client relationships.
+ most personal situations.

C2 is not the appropriate style

+ when, after multiple attempts on your part to be collaborative, the other side refuses to work with you (classic C1).
+ if you are asked to do something immoral, unethical, or illegal.

> **PROFESSIONAL NEGOTIATING TIP**

Collaborative negotiators must recognize situations where C2 is not appropriate and shift to C1. Stand firm.

As we have said, this is a great style for win-win negotiations, and using it properly will lead to smoother, more satisfying deals and repeat business. As we move through this book, we will discuss techniques designed to make your negotiations more collaborative. It is critical, however, that you learn how to determine when the other party is genuinely collaborating with you. Sometimes buyers will appear to be working with you when they are really trying to pick your pocket. When this happens, you need to shift into another mode (usually a "soft" C1) to avoid giving away the store.

Negotiation tips for dealing with C2's include the following:

+ Let them know that you are looking for a win-win too.
+ Focus on the relationship and the issues.

Negotiation tips for you if you are a C2 include the following:

+ Recognize that not everyone else negotiates the way you do.
+ Beware of C1's disguising themselves as C2's.
+ Remember that sometimes you will have to shift to a "soft" C1 to be more effective.

C3: Concede

We often see this style in salespeople. They are so focused on building the relationship with their buyers that they sometimes give away a lot more than they should. Buyers know this and will use it to their advantage.

How often have you heard a salesperson say (or you said), "I had to give them X, Y, and Z, but now we've got our foot in the door, and we're going to do a lot of business with these guys"?

Maybe. The problem with this style and this approach is if you aren't careful, you will set an expectation with the other party that every time she asks you for something, she is going to get it. She thinks that doing business with you is going to be a lot of fun. And you are going to be facing a tough choice pretty soon: either you are going to be stuck with an unprofitable account, or you are going to have to stop giving things away.

If C3 is your natural style or you are using it, particularly early on in a relationship, you need to be extremely careful. The key is to let the buyer know that you are making an exception to your usual business practices in order to remove an obstacle to doing business. You can say something like, "It isn't our standard practice to do this, but if all that is stopping us from writing this order is the credit for unsold seasonal goods, I can make that problem go away—if this new order is 20 percent higher than the last order."

C3 is a good style to use

+ if you have created a problem for the client.
+ if something relatively small is in the way of the deal.
+ when what you have to give up is minor compared to the upside business potential.

C3 is not appropriate

+ when you are asked to concede on something major.
+ when you get nothing in return for the concession.
+ when issues are nonnegotiable (legal, moral, safety, etc.).

Remember, the C3 style will get you into trouble when (a) you set the expectation that you will routinely give in to demands for concessions, or (b) you make the concessions without asking for something in return.

If you have to concede in order to establish the business relationship or get the order, make sure the other party knows that the concession is an exception to your usual practices and that it is a condition for moving the process forward.

Negotiation tips for dealing with C3's include the following:

+ If they are giving you things, keep asking.
+ If they don't ask for anything in return, keep asking.

> PROFESSIONAL NEGOTIATING TIP

If C3 is your style, you need to be very careful not to create an expectation that you will always give in to client demands.

Negotiation tips for you if you are a C3 include the following:

+ Always make concessions conditional.
+ Manage the other party's expectation of when and how you will concede.
+ Never use this style with C1's; move to C1 to avoid getting crushed.

C4: Compromise

C4's don't really like to negotiate. They would rather be doing something else. The beauty of this style is that it is quick to reach a conclusion. Let's just split the difference, meet me halfway, and we have a deal.

Sounds fair, doesn't it? The problem is that if the differences are significant, one or both parties may walk away unhappy with their deal. In order for this to work, both sides have to give up some of what they want. If someone feels that he gave up too much or that the other party didn't give up enough, then he starts looking for a way out. This isn't good.

C4 is a good style to use

+ if the differences are relatively minor and the result is acceptable to both parties.
+ if you are running out of time.
+ if you have exhausted all of the obvious alternatives.

C4 is not a good style to use

+ if the differences are major.
+ if the outcome of a split is unacceptable to one or both parties.

+ if the issues are nonnegotiable for your company (see above).

+ if you have time to look for a win-win solution.

Another problem with this style is that if you aren't careful, a skilled negotiator can get you to split more than once (see Chapter 5). If you need to compromise, try to make it a condition for closing the deal. Say, "If I'm able to do that, can we go ahead and write this order up?"

Note: don't get confused between a compromise and a concession.

Using Styles in Negotiations

STYLE	APPROPRIATE	INAPPROPRIATE
CONQUER	ONE-TIME SALES. NO COMPETITION.* THEY WILL NOT COLLABORATE.	LONG-TERM RELATIONSHIP. THEY HAVE A CLEAR CHOICE EARLY IN THE NEGOTIATIONS.
COLLABORATE	SOLVING A PROBLEM. BOTH SIDES NEED SOMETHING. YOU HAVE TIME TO ARRIVE AT A SOLUTION. YOU WANT TO USE THE NEGOTIATION TO BUILD THE RELATIONSHIP.	AFTER TRYING, THE OTHER SIDE WILL NOT COLLABORATE. WHAT THEY ARE ASKING FOR VIOLATES PERSONAL ETHICS OR CORPORATE VALUES.
CONCEDE	YOU OR YOUR COMPANY HAS CAUSED A PROBLEM. THE ISSUE AND/OR VALUE IS MINOR.	FIRST TIME NEGOTIATIONS (SETS BAD PRECEDENT) YOU HAVE TIME TO EXPLORE THROUGH COLLABORATION.
COMPROMISE	THE ISSUE AND VALUE ARE MINOR. THERE IS NO MORE TIME, AND THE SPLIT IS OF LITTLE VALUE.	WHEN YOU HAVE MORE TIME TO COLLABORATE.

* Be careful. You may have competition someday.

In a compromise, both parties are giving up something in order to reach an agreement. In a concession, only one party concedes on a point.

Negotiation tips for dealing with C4's include the following:

+ Look for the win-win solution first.
+ Make sure that the differences are small and the results are acceptable.
+ Clearly define the issues on which you will not compromise.

Negotiation tips for you if you are a C4 include the following:

+ Take the time to look for a creative solution to important issues.
+ If you have to compromise, make it a condition of closing the deal.
+ Compromise only once per issue.

> ### ➤ PROFESSIONAL NEGOTIATING TIP

If C4 is your style, resist the temptation to compromise quickly. If you have the time, explore other alternatives and avoid leaving anything on the table.

Complete the following exercises to test your understanding of the use of styles.

Styles Exercises

Try your skill at recognizing different negotiation styles in these two practice exercises. The correct answers will be given at the end of the exercise.

Exercise #1: Carol is one of your favorite contract suppliers. You have known her for more than ten years, and she has always been willing to work with you. Carol values the relationship that she has with you and your company. In the past, when contract negotiations have been really tough, Carol has always made sure that you got everything you needed in the agreement.

Based on this information, what is Carol's negotiation style?

(a) Conquer
(b) Collaborate
(c) Concede
(d) Compromise

Exercise #2: Dave is another of your favorite suppliers. Negotiations with Dave always seem to produce what he calls "fair results." Whenever the negotiation gets stuck, Dave looks for middle ground where the two of you can "split the difference" and walk away happy.

Based on this information, what is Dave's negotiation style?

(a) Conquer
(b) Collaborate
(c) Concede
(d) Compromise

Exercise #1: (c). Carol places more value on the relationship than the substance of the issues being negotiated.

Exercise #2: (d). Dave values the relationship and the substance of the issues being negotiated. However, he may look too quickly for middle ground, which could result in not satisfying the needs of either party.

Summary

Good negotiators and good salespeople know their own negotiating styles, and they can quickly size up the style that the other party is using. They know that there is no one "best" style. Based on the situation, they will use the style that is most likely to yield the best results.

Recognizing and reacting to styles accordingly will make your negotiations smoother, more productive, and less stressful.

CHAPTER 3

DEALING WITH TOUGH NEGOTIATORS

Some years ago, we encountered a salesperson with a typical story. He had submitted a large order for capital equipment to his company. A review found that the order was seriously underpriced. In fact, it was at least 10 percent below the level that either the salesperson or his regional manager had the authority to discount. When the regional manager's boss called the salesperson to see what was going on, the salesperson launched into a litany of the bad things that the buyer had done to him:

+ He was rude.
+ He was profane.
+ He screamed at him.
+ He waved the competition's offer in his face.
+ He refused to pay any more than the amount on the purchase order, and so on.

When the boss pointed out that the salesperson wasn't authorized to quote the prices on the purchase order (PO), the salesperson said in exasperation, "You don't understand. This guy is a jerk!"

To which the boss replied, "Jack, we don't have a special price list for jerks."

The salesperson knew this, of course, but he had decided that it would be easier to accept the crummy deal from his customer and to finesse it through the company than to go toe-to-toe with the buyer and get the deal that he should have gotten.

Sound familiar?

It is quite common for buyers to use intimidation, hostility, and emotion as tactics to throw sellers off balance. Buyers use them, like most tactics, because they work. Quite often, they are trying to get you emotional because they know that you are more likely to do something irrational if you lose your temper.

> **➤ PROFESSIONAL NEGOTIATING TIP**
>
> A mad negotiator is a bad negotiator. If you find yourself losing your temper or getting emotional, you have to do something to get yourself under control. For tips on how to do this, read on.

In this chapter, we will discuss techniques that we have developed over the years specifically designed to deal with the bully, the screamer, and the emotional or hostile buyer. Sometimes things happen that make even reasonable customers get angry, and you need to deal with them in order to get things back on track.

Not every technique will work every time, but good negotiators use these skill sets when the action gets intense.

Let Them Blow Off Steam

Did you ever walk into a meeting where you knew the other party was just waiting to unload on you about something? Maybe there has been a problem with a shipment or a billing error or whatever, but you know that the person is going to blast you just as soon as the meeting starts.

We have found that the best strategy in these cases is to let these people blast away. There's not much point in trying to head them off at the pass with a preemptive strike. They are going to unload on you, and they aren't going to be in any mood to listen to you until they do.

It's also important to let them get it all out. Don't try to debate them point by point as they go through whatever is bothering them; just let them rip. If you have to say anything at all, say something noncommittal like, "I can see why you might feel that way," or "Yes, I see that this is an important issue to you." In other words, let them know that you are listening and paying attention to their "ravings" without necessarily agreeing with them. You haven't said that they are right and you are wrong.

Encourage them to get all of the issues on the table. When they stop pounding you, ask, "Is that everything?" Quite often, they will say no and bring up two or three more things that are bothering them. You can't begin to address their issues until you know what they are. Sometimes the issues that you have to dig the hardest for are the real sources of the problem.

Remember, you are not debating them on their complaints, nor are you agreeing with them. You are simply acknowledging what they are saying and encouraging them to be thorough. You might even take notes to show them that you are taking their position seriously. You need to resist the temptation to jump in and defend yourself and/or your company. Doing this will generally lead to an escalation of tension and emotion, which is the exact opposite of what you are trying to accomplish.

Okay, so they have blasted you for fifteen or twenty minutes, and finally all of their grievances are on the table. Now what? It is a very normal response to get angry or emotional during this kind of a tirade. Quite often, the buyer is hoping for this response (see the Professional Negotiating Tip at the beginning of this chapter). It is critical that you engage the other party, not on an emotional level, but on a rational basis. No matter how angry or unpleasant the person has been up to this point, you need to get your emotions under control and respond in a calm and professional manner. The best way to ensure that this happens is to . . .

Take a Break

Taking a break is one of the most powerful tools in a good negotiator's bag of tricks. Taking a break will allow you to

+ calm down.
+ develop a strategy to deal with the situation.
+ break negative momentum.
+ regain control of the agenda.
+ change the emotional level of the meeting.
+ shift the power in the room.

If you find yourself getting upset, take a break.
If your strategy isn't working, take a break.
If you are getting beaten on the issues, take a break.
If you get blindsided by something, take a break.
If momentum is going against you, take a break.
We'll explain how to do this in just a moment.

Recently an executive from Vistage came to a workshop. (Vistage was formerly known as TEC, The Executive Committee). She arranged to bring a number of her staff to another workshop that we were doing in her area. Their company operates an in-bound call center. When we were discussing these techniques in the follow-up class, she stopped us to tell this story:

A week or so before the class, she was pursuing a potentially big new client. She had made arrangements for the client to test the effectiveness of her phone people with a small-scale project. The executive and the prospective client met later to discuss the results. The client opened the meeting with a litany of complaints about the quality of the phone operators. According to him, they were

+ too slow to pick up the phone (four rings).
+ too "ethnic" sounding.
+ not enthusiastic enough about his products.
+ too loud.
+ not loud enough.

It was obvious to the executive that the client was trying to bait her with a lot of nitpicky complaints. Fortunately for her company, she had been through our workshop. So she listened politely to all of the client's comments and criticisms. She waited until he had gotten everything out on the table, and then she said that she needed a ten-minute break.

She went down the hall and collected her thoughts. She was mildly irritated by the client's whining, but she didn't fall for the tactic. In fact, she didn't react to it at all. What she did was to get herself calm and collected. After ten minutes, she walked back into the conference room, looked the client straight in the eye, and said, "When would you like us to start?"

The client was so surprised and off balance that he started fumbling with his papers. When he finally spoke, it was to begin the discussion of when the call center would start on his project full-time.

Another quick story:

A regional manager of a large consumer products company was in one of our workshops. Two weeks later, he was called to the home office for a meeting with the CEO of his company. He told us later that the meeting was not going well, as the CEO and the CFO were talking about changing the entire sales force structure. After listening to this discussion for quite a while, the regional manager said, "I really need to go down the hall. Mind if I take a quick break?" (Remember, this is an internal meeting with his boss's boss.) The CEO seemed a little stunned but said sure. The regional manager came back in about ten minutes. He said he couldn't believe the change in both the CEO's and the CFO's attitudes. The first thing out of the CEO's mouth was, "We were talking while you were gone, and we think we need to get your input into how we might do this. Maybe we have been doing too much talking." The regional manager hadn't said a word on entering the room. That's what we are talking about—taking a break can change the power in the room!

These are just a couple of examples of how and why this technique can work for you.

Taking a break will not only give you the opportunity to calm down and regroup; it will also give everyone time to relax. When you walk back into the meeting room and say, "Okay, now let's get started," who's got the momentum? You do! Who's in charge of the agenda? You are!

So we are in agreement that it's a good thing to take breaks. How do you do it? If you are negotiating as a part of a team, it is relatively easy to call for a break. You just say something like, "We need to step outside and talk this over. We'll be right back." And you walk out. (Please take your notes or at least cover them up when you step out.)

That's great, but what if you are in there all by yourself? You've got no one to step outside with. If anything, breaks are even more important in one-on-one meetings than they are in team situations, so you need to know how to do it. Here's what we recommend: when you aren't happy with the way things are going and you know that you need to regroup, you say, "We've been at this for a while now, and we've still got some issues left to cover. I need to step down the hall for a moment."

So what does that mean in virtually all cultures?

It means, "I need a bathroom break." Now, has anyone (since you've been an adult) ever said no to you? Unlikely. Besides, you aren't asking permission. You are making a statement. Say it, get up, and walk out.

We have found this approach to be better than saying, "I need to make a phone call." Why? Because having to make a call implies that you don't have the authority or the expertise to deal with the situation yourself. That costs you power.

Take whatever time you need to cool down, adjust your strategy, think up alternatives or whatever, and then go back to the meeting room. You walk in, sit down, and say, "Okay, let's get started."

Remember, this is a game! If you walk back to the meeting room after a break and the other party isn't there, are you going to go in and sit down and wait?

No!

You want to be the one who enters last and starts the meeting. If she isn't there, (a) wait in the hall for her to get back, or (b) leave her a note saying you'll be back in a few minutes. You want to be the one in charge when the meeting resumes.

Good negotiators take lots of breaks.

> ➤ PROFESSIONAL NEGOTIATING TIP
>
> The sales side underutilizes breaks. Taking a break may mean the difference between a successful outcome and a failed negotiation.

Go to the Balcony

As we mentioned previously, it's easy during an intense negotiation to become emotional or get caught up in the momentum of the discussion. It's also very dangerous. Good negotiators know that to be effective, they have to keep their emotions in check and maintain perspective on what's going on.

Here's how we recommend you do that. Make yourself a note that says, "Go to the balcony." Place the note so that you can see it when you glance at your other meeting prep materials.

What does "going to the balcony" mean? Good negotiators train themselves to *mentally* step away from the table every few minutes. We stress the word *mentally* because, physically, you are still sitting at the table negotiating. Mentally, however, you step away and climb a couple of invisible stairs and look down on the parties (including yourself) who are sitting there working on the deal.

As you are looking down on them, ask yourself these questions:

+ Who's winning?
+ Who's losing?
+ Who's getting frustrated and/or angry?
+ Whose strategy is working?
+ Who's on the defensive?
+ Do I need to do anything differently?

Now, if your strategy is working and you are scoring points and rolling along, what are you going to do? Keep it up!

But if your strategy isn't working, if you are getting emotional, or if you are getting creamed, what are you going to do? Take a break! Regroup. Change your tactics. Don't just sit there and keep getting creamed!

The point here is that unless you make a conscious effort to maintain your perspective, it is way too easy to get swept up in the heat of the moment and do something you'll regret later. When momentum is going against you, you need to recognize it early and do something to break it. Otherwise, by the time you realize that you are in trouble, it is too late to do anything about it.

Good negotiators, like good card players, are constantly monitoring the situation from a detached, third-party perspective in order to be able to react quickly when things start looking bad for the home team. If you don't force yourself to do this, you can get carried away and end up somewhere you don't want to be.

Focus on the Problem Together

Sometimes you make a lot of progress, and then one issue hangs everything up. Let's say that you and the buyer have agreed on price, terms, and order size, but you hit a brick wall when it comes to the delivery date. The buyer wants the product in four weeks, and you can't get it there in less than eight weeks—a recipe for an instant impasse.

What generally happens in this case is that both parties spend a lot of time explaining why their time frame is what it is and why it has to be that way. If you aren't careful, things may become emotional and personal. In other words, each party begins to identify the other as the problem. This isn't good.

> ➤ PROFESSIONAL NEGOTIATING TIP
>
> Be tough on the issues and soft on the people. Use techniques to focus attention on the issues and away from you!

We use a deceptively simple technique when this happens. As soon as we hit the deadlock, we say, "Look, the problem isn't you and it isn't me. It's this delivery date issue. Let's write it [delivery date] on this flip chart and focus on coming up with a solution." We write the problem on the chart, and then we walk back to the table. If possible, we sit on the same side of the table as our client, and together, we brainstorm ideas to see if we can figure out a solution. If a flip chart isn't available, we write the issue on a piece of paper and put it in front of both parties.

See how collaborative we are now? The problem isn't us or them; it's over there, and we are working on it together. Doing this may sound silly, but it works.

One final note: Occasionally we see salespeople almost get this one right and then blow it at the last minute. Sometimes they will write the problem on the board and then stand there. This isn't good because they are still identifying themselves with the issue. Sit down, face the issue together, and work out the problem with your client.

Reverse the Ridiculous

Making a demand or an offer that is patently ridiculous can be the other party's tactic to force you to say no early in the negotiation. From that point on, you are looking for a way to say yes to something in order to seem reasonable and collaborative. In fact, you may agree to something that you shouldn't because you don't want to say no again.

A better response to an unrealistic demand is to say, "Put yourself in my shoes, Bob. If I accept an offer that is 25 percent below market, how am I going to look to my boss?" Or you can say, "Your offer is at least 25 percent below market. How would you feel if I brought in a quote that was 25 percent above what it should be?" or "We both know that

I'd get fired if I brought home an order priced like that. Let's talk about what we can do."

Consider the Use of Humor—with Caution

Humor can sometimes be very effective in defusing a tense situation. It can be risky, though, if you don't know the other party well or you aren't adept at humor.

For example, we recently submitted a training proposal to the HR director of a Fortune 500 company. The project involved training more than one thousand salespeople. The HR Director leafed through the document quickly and then went to the back page; you know, the one with the numbers. When she looked at the bottom line, she performed a classic "flinch" (see Chapter 5). The author sat quietly for a moment and then asked, "Too low?" The director looked shocked for a bit and then broke into a smile and began to discuss the timing of the project. She knew that our figure was reasonable given the scope of work that she wanted, and we knew that it was consistent with what she had budgeted.

In this case, we had a high confidence level that the director would respond favorably to humor. Had we not known her as well, we would have ignored the flinch and waited for her to speak first.

The point here is that good negotiators are constantly aware of the emotional level of the meeting and how things are going. When things aren't going according to plan, they act quickly to break the momentum and change strategies before they get into trouble. Effective salespeople do the same thing.

You will be amazed at how much easier it is to do good deals when you avoid and defuse emotion on both sides of the table.

CHAPTER 4

SETTING THE TONE

Believe it or not, you can make your negotiations more productive by doing a few very basic things at the beginning of your meeting. In fact, these things are so basic that many smart people gloss right over them and make their lives more difficult than they need to be.

Dress Right

What you wear to the meeting can affect how comfortable the other party is with you. Ideally you should try to dress just slightly better than the client. If the dress code is business casual, you should shoot for the dressier end of that definition. If the client wears business attire, then by all means, you should wear a business suit. What you are trying to accomplish here is to build what we call equal business standing (in a nonverbal way) so that your clothing is saying, "We think like you and we do business like you."

Note: Equal business standing means that you have created an impression that says, "I am a professional. I know my business. I belong here. I have products and programs that can help you."

Of course, your company's dress code policy may dictate what you wear in all situations, so you may not always have flexibility.

Since dress codes are all over the map these days (and subject to change on short notice), it's a good idea to call ahead if you aren't sure of the norm where you will be meeting. You can ask the person with whom you will be meeting, the person's assistant, or even the switchboard operator. All you need to say is something like, "I'll be meeting with Ms. XXX on Tuesday, and I was wondering, what kind of dress code do you have at XYZ Corp.?" People are generally glad to help.

> ➤ PROFESSIONAL NEGOTIATING TIP
> Establishing equal business standing is a critical step in setting the appropriate tone for a negotiation with your customer.

Carry the Right Stuff

Just like your clothes, the things that you carry into the meeting will make a statement about who you are. You want to be sure that you are sending the right message. For higher-level negotiations, we recommend a high-quality leather portfolio with enough room in it for a couple of file folders, a legal pad, your calendar, a calculator, business cards, and, of course, your notes and planning sheets for the meeting.

What you want to avoid is one of those big salesperson's catalog cases (we used to call them schlepper cases). They make anyone look like a peddler. That's not the message you want to send about who you are and what your status is.

The same concept holds true for computer bags, AV aids, catalogs, and so on. These can be great sales tools, but if you aren't careful, you can look like a nomad staggering under a load of props. Carry only what you need. Keep it neat and organized so that you can quickly find what you are looking for. Rummaging around in your briefcase does not reassure the other party that you are a professional.

Watch Your Nonverbals

Your body language (see Chapter 6) should reinforce, not conflict with, the image you want to convey. The image is that you are a poised professional who is prepared, relaxed, and looking forward to this meeting.

You want to make eye contact during the introductions. Stick with a firm but not crushing handshake. Stand until everyone begins to sit, and then, when you sit, lean slightly forward in an attentive manner.

Everything about your body language should say:

+ I am a professional.
+ I am prepared.
+ I am looking forward to this meeting.
+ I belong at this table.

One final note on nonverbals: If you are meeting at your client's place of business, you will probably have to wear one of those annoying security badges while you are in the building. Everyone does these days. The problem is, that sends a message you don't want to send. Think about it. While you are doing everything you can to create an atmosphere that is collaborative and collegial, that "visitor" badge around your neck is sending a subliminal message to the client that screams: "Alien! Alien! Be careful with this person, because he isn't one of us."

Since you can't walk around most places without the badge, what are you going to do? We recommend attaching it somewhere near your waist. Clip it on your belt or to a side pocket on your jacket. That way, when you sit down, the badge is hidden by the edge of the table or desk, and the subliminal message goes away.

This may seem to be a very small detail, but that's the whole point of this chapter. These small things add up to a powerful nonverbal message. Sometimes what you aren't saying speaks a whole lot louder than what you are.

Present Opening Comments

It's time to open the meeting. If you look across the table, you might see grim faces and stiff body language. The atmosphere in the room might be full of tension. These people are geared up for a war!

As we will discuss in other sections of this book, many people approach a negotiation as they would a fight. They become anxious, combative, distrustful, and distant. This attitude doesn't set the stage for a good collaborative meeting, does it?

A primary reason people walk in with this attitude is that they are afraid others will take advantage of them in the negotiation. They need to do a good job for their company, and they don't want to lose face if things don't turn out well.

What you say in the first few minutes of the meeting can go a long way to (a) relax the tension and create a more positive feeling in the room, or (b) confirm to them that they are indeed going to be in a battle with you. Obviously (a) is better most of the time, so how do you do it?

We recommend that you open with a statement like this:

> We have been looking forward to meeting with you today. This
> project is very important to us, and we know that it is important to you

as well. In thinking about how we might work together on this, we have tried to look at it from your perspective as well as our own. In looking at the issues, we have found several areas where we seem to already match up and other areas where we are close. We have some interesting ideas about how this deal could work for both of us, and we are sure that you have given it some thought as well. We are convinced that there is a way we can make this project a win-win for both of us. One more thing: I will take the notes of our discussion and send them back to you. Okay? Great, let's get started. An area that we both seem to match up in is . . .

What did that accomplish? Let's examine what you said and what you are really saying:

+ "We have been looking forward to meeting with you today."

We are glad to be here! Notice you didn't say, "Thank you for making the time to meet with us." Your time is just as valuable as theirs (another opportunity for equal business standing)!

+ "This project is very important to us, and we know that it is important to you as well."

We take this meeting seriously, and we know that you do too. We aren't here to waste anyone's time.

+ "In thinking about how we might work together on this, we have tried to look at it from your perspective as well as our own."

You have just increased the power meter on your side! Imagine what's running through their minds if they haven't thought about this meeting beforehand and you are telling them that you are prepared! You also are saying, "We aren't in this to grab as much as we can for ourselves. We have thought about this deal from your side as well as our own, and we have tried to think about what might be important to both sides."

+ "We have some interesting ideas about how this deal could work for both of us, and we are sure that you have given it some thought as well."

We have prepared for this meeting. We have come up with ideas and suggestions that we think will benefit both sides. In addition to that, we are open to whatever ideas you have.

+ "We are convinced that there is a way we can make this project a win-win for both of us."

We want everyone to be happy with the outcome, and we are open-minded and ready to work with you to make it happen.

+ "One more thing: I will take the notes of our discussion and send them back to you."

Watch the power meter again. It has just increased more on your side. Writing the notes for the meeting gives you additional control over the interpretation of the discussion and, thus, more power.

+ "Let's get started."

So let's tackle this thing together!

Obviously the exact words you use will be different for every situation, but the goal is the same. You want to reassure the people on the buyer's side that you are prepared, open-minded, ready to work with them to come up with a good solution, and interested in their ideas as well as your own.

Since most of the other people they deal with won't open a meeting in this way, you have just set yourself apart from your competition and (we hope) created an atmosphere in the room that is more conducive to the sharing of information and ideas and is less confrontational.

> **➤ PROFESSIONAL NEGOTIATING TIP**
>
> Setting the tone properly can establish more power for the salesperson as well as a collaborative atmosphere.

How will you know that your approach worked?

Simple. If you do a good job of setting the tone, you will see everyone begin to relax. Shoulders will come down, facial expressions will soften, and the tension level in the room will lessen. You have set the stage for a more collaborative negotiation.

One word of caution: If the meeting is at the client's location, in his or her office or conference room, the client may very well want to open the meeting. That's fine. Let the client say what he wants to say, and then you deliver your opening statement.

You will be amazed at how something so simple can alter the dynamics of the meeting. Good negotiators pay attention to detail.

It's a good idea to practice your opening statement a few times when you are preparing for the negotiation. The goal is to communicate your collaborative intentions while keeping the power meter high on your end without sounding phony or canned. Try it out on a colleague to make sure that it sounds the way it did to you when you practiced it in your head.

CHAPTER 5

OVERCOMING THE BAD THINGS BUYERS LEARN IN "SCHOOL"

IT'S A SAFE BET THAT AS YOU ARE READING THIS CHAPTER, somewhere there is a room full of aspiring purchasing agents being trained in the black arts of buyer tactics. Years ago, such training was the sole province of the largest organizations. Today, however, a buyer training program is a routine part of the orientation program for many small to medium-sized firms.

Why would otherwise ethical, responsible corporations train their employees in how to be disingenuous and manipulative? Because it works. As pressure mounts on all businesses to protect margins, the purchasing function is seen as the first line of defense for the bottom line. Buyer tactics are ruses, ploys, and stratagems that are used to gain leverage in negotiations with suppliers. Quite often they are designed to keep the vendor off balance, defensive, nervous, and disorganized.

As we stated early on in the book—and it is worth repeating—companies know that salespeople are trained to develop relationships with their clients. Salespeople are taught to nurture these relationships and use them to help sell their products and services. The client companies are worried that these relationships might color the objectivity of their purchasing groups and prevent them from going for the jugular in pricing negotiations.

To counter this possibility, many companies will go to great lengths to prevent their buyers and supplier salespeople from getting too comfortable with one another. Some companies change buying responsibilities every few months so that salespeople are always calling on someone new. Most companies have cut way back on the kinds of gifts that their purchasing people can accept; long lunches, trips, and tickets to ball games are going the way of the blue eyeshadow.

In addition to these measures, many companies teach their purchasing staffs how to use tactics to disrupt and derail sales presentations. Many, many tactics have evolved over the years, but all have the same objective: concession.

> **PROFESSIONAL NEGOTIATING TIP**

Tactics are designed to gain additional leverage or an unfair advantage in a business negotiation. In truth, all tactics are used to gain a concession from the other side.

Properly applied, tactics can be devastatingly effective. There are far more tactics floating around than we have room to deal with in this book. In this chapter, however, we will identify and discuss thirteen of the most common buyer tactics. More important, we will outline the appropriate countertactic for each one.

Knowledge is power, and, in all cases, being prepared for these tactics removes the panic and allows the educated salesperson to recognize and deal with buyer tactics smoothly and professionally. If you have been selling for any length of time, you will recognize some or maybe all of these tactics.

Here we go.

Tactic #1: The Nibble

You will usually see this tactic at the very end of the negotiation. Typically it will appear when all of the major points have been agreed to and the buyer is getting ready to sign off on the deal. As the buyer is literally, or figuratively, getting ready to put her pen on the dotted line, she looks up and says something like this:

> "All of our major partners have agreed to ninety-day payment terms. That's okay, isn't it?"
>> or
> "This does include free freight, right?"
>> or
> "Why don't you throw in a spare parts kit at no charge?"

You get the idea. A nibble is a small bite, and the point of the nibble is to catch the salesperson at the point of maximum vulnerability and to use his eagerness to get the deal done to wring a last concession or two out of him.

From the salesperson's point of view, this is a huge problem. If he says yes, he is giving away something that he hadn't planned to give away. This could get him in hot water back at the office. On the other hand, if he says no, he may blow the deal!

Unfortunately it gets worse. Assuming the poor, pressured sales-person takes a deep breath and agrees to the nibble, whatever it was, the buyer has almost certainly been trained to come back with a request for something else. Yikes!

Countertactic

As with most negotiating situations, the key to this one is planning. It is a good idea to assume that you will be "nibbled" at the end of every significant negotiation. Great negotiators know this and put together a list of counternibbles. In other words, you make a list, in advance, of things that you might ask for if you get nibbled.

Let's revisit the scenario:

Purchasing Manager: This does include ninety-day terms, right?

Salesperson: If I'm able to do that, could you give me a 40 per-cent [versus the usual 20 percent] down payment?

Notice that the salesperson hasn't said yes or no. By asking for some-thing of roughly equal value in return, the salesperson deflects the request without giving anything away or causing the buyer to lose face.

Purchasing Manager: Never mind. Let's just do the deal as it stands.

This countertactic is so effective because, by definition, a nibble isn't important to the buyer. If it were, it would already be in the deal. The buyer is just trying to use the seller's eagerness to get another concession or two. When the seller asks for a quid pro quo, the buyer will generally revert to the terms of the original deal because that's what was important to her in the first place. And if the buyer says okay to the quid pro quo and if the seller planned it well, both sides get something they wanted!

> ➤ PROFESSIONAL NEGOTIATING TIP
>
> It is difficult to come up with appropriate counternibbles on the spur of the moment. It is much easier to put together a list of four or five potential counternibbles while you are planning for the meeting.

Tactic #2: The Bogey

A bogey is a blip or a target on a radar screen. As a negotiating tactic, a bogey is usually a number thrown out by the buyer. It will look something like this: "We really like doing business with your company. You've got great products and services, and we want you to get this project. [Here it comes!] The problem is, we have only X to spend."

Naturally whatever X equals is less than what you want to get for this particular package of goods and/or services. What makes this tactic work is that it seems so collaborative and friendly. They like you! They want to do business with you! They just can't afford to pay you what your products are worth.

It's amazing how many salespeople will fall for this one and go back to their companies with a whole list of reasons why they should take the deal. Usually their arguments center on "getting our foot in the door" or "keeping those other guys out."

That's the goal of this tactic: to get the salesperson working on behalf of the buyer to help justify lowball pricing.

Countertactic

The first thing that you want to do when the buyer throws out a bogey is to test it. Is the bogey real? That is, does the company really have only X to spend, or is the buyer just fishing for a low price? Usually a few good open-ended *why* questions can shed light on the truth. For example, the salesperson might ask:

"Where did that number come from?"

or

"Is that your total budget for this project, or is there additional funding available if we can show you a great return on your investment [ROI]?"

or

"When does your fiscal year end?"

You get the idea. If, after questioning, you determine that the bogey was just a ploy and that there is more money to be had, then you continue selling your value proposition. On the other hand, if the bogey is a real budget number, then you've got work to do.

At this point you want to change the shape of the deal in some way in order to fit the buyer's budget without hurting your own margins. You can do this by

+ changing the scope of the deal. You can adjust the scope of your quotation to fit the client's budget.
+ changing the timing. Find out what your client's budget year looks like, and then see if you can do your project in phases that coincide with new budget-funding periods.
+ having alternatives. Offer the buyer more than one way to get the job done. Any time that you have a client trying to choose

between several of your options instead of between you and a competitor, you are ahead of the game.

Don't fall for the bogey trap. Just because your customer wants to spend only X doesn't mean that you are under any obligation to underprice your products.

Tactic #3: The Squeeze

We have taught negotiation skills all over the world, and we have seen this tactic used everywhere. In English, it boils down to the same eight words: "You will have to do better than that!"

The implication here is that there is no point in continuing the discussion unless you, as the seller, make some kind of a concession. The reason it is so effective is that most salespeople cannot resist the temptation to ask, "How much better do I have to do?"

This is exactly the wrong thing to say! If you ask how much better, the buyer will almost certainly tell you. He will throw out a number ($10,000, or 15 percent, for example), and then you will have to find a way to deal with that number. You are no longer talking about value or benefits; you are haggling over price. Worse, you are essentially negotiating against yourself.

Countertactic

In this situation you, as the seller, are far better off to avoid the trap and say something like this: "Our offer is very competitive with what we are seeing in the marketplace for a deal like this. Why don't you tell me a little more about what you are comparing us to?" This line of questioning will allow you to continue to sell value or payback. It will also give you the opportunity to point out the important ways in which your proposal differs from your competitor's.

Don't take the bait! Never, ever ask, "How much better do I have to do?"

> ➤ PROFESSIONAL NEGOTIATING TIP
>
> Some tactics such as the squeeze are created so the seller actually starts negotiating with herself!

Tactic #4: Time Pressure

This tactic will generally appear in one of two forms.

You are making an out-of-town sales call. You walk into your client's office, and after an exchange of pleasantries, the client asks, "What time is your flight home?" You say, "Four o'clock."

The client then says, "Great. Why don't we show you around, give you a plant tour, show you what we do here, and let you meet some of the staff." You agree and spend the next hour and a half walking around. Then the client says, "It's almost noon. Why don't we grab a bite and then come back and talk about this deal?" You agree and off you go to lunch.

When you get back, you look at your watch and realize that it is almost one o'clock, and you haven't even begun to talk about your project. In your mind, you start picturing the long lines at airport security and all of the complications if you miss your flight. You've got a rental car to refuel and drop off. You need to be on the road in about thirty minutes, and you are just now opening your briefcase.

You've got time pressure!

The farther away from home you are, the more effective this tactic is. The buyer's goal, of course, is to eat up any time available for a discussion of your project's merits and value. The buyer wants to leave you with just enough time to shoot her your best price and then have you bolt out the door.

A business friend told us about a project a few years ago in which a Japanese company used this tactic effectively. The seller, an American construction company, had a team in Japan for two weeks to discuss the terms of a project to build a chemical plant outside Tokyo. The Japanese played host to them with all of the hospitality for which they are famous. For ten days, the Americans were driven around to see all of the sights: pagodas, shrines, Mount Fuji, karaoke bars, the works! On the eleventh day they realized that they had a very complicated deal to put together and not nearly enough time to get it done.

They got the business, but they left too much on the table and sold the deal at too low a price. They were victims of time pressure. By the time they had all of the technical challenges worked out, they had no time left to justify the margins that they typically received. They just stuck in a lowball price and sprinted for the airport.

Countertactic

The best way to deflect this kind of time pressure is not to acknowledge it. In answer to the question "What time is your flight?" you reply something like this: "This is an important deal for us. I will be here as long as I need to ensure that you have all the information you need to make a good decision."

But, you say, sometimes you really do have a plane to catch and other appointments to keep. Of course, you do.

The point is not that you don't have time pressure. We all have it. The point is that you don't admit you have it.

When the client says, "Let's take a plant tour," you say, "I'm looking forward to seeing your shop and meeting your people, but the main reason I'm here is to discuss this deal, and I think we should do that first. Then we can use whatever time we have left to do the tour."

In this way, you have politely but firmly declined to participate in the time-pressure game.

Here's another way that buyers can use time pressure on you. Let's say that you are driving down the road, minding your own business, and your cell phone rings. It's your big new client, and she says, "I'm glad I caught you. We are getting ready to go into a meeting and make a decision on the ACME project, and I need to be sure that I've got your best and final offer. Are you sure you've given me your best price?"

Holy mackerel, the ACME project! You don't have the proposal with you, but you are pretty sure that you had an extra 5 percent or so in there just in case you needed it. This will knock the heck out of your commission, but you don't want to lose the deal, so you give the discount. The buyer thanks you and says she'll let you know what happens.

What usually happens is that the buyer will call you back in two or three weeks and tell you that the company is getting ready to move on ACME and she wants you to come in and discuss your proposal. In other words, there was no meeting to decide on the deal. You have been had!

The whole point of this tactic, like most of the others, is to knock you off balance. By catching you unprepared and scaring you with the fiction of a looming decision, the buyer was trying to stampede you into hastily shooting from the hip and lowering your price.

Countertactic

The truth is that most companies don't make snap decisions on significant expenditures. They follow a procedure and a process. In this case, it is essential that you keep your composure and buy yourself some time to think.

You want to say something like this: "Wow, you caught me off guard. I was in the middle of something else. I need a few minutes to review our proposal and ensure that you have our best deal. Give me a cell number or the extension of someone sitting outside your conference room, and I will call back after I have had a chance to review your file."

Now you have time to take a few deep breaths, examine your offer, and think about how you want to respond to the buyer. The point here is not to panic and do something that you will regret later. You are much better off making a decision on what to do about your proposal if you can do so calmly and rationally instead of off the top of your head and under pressure.

There is an element of power in this tactic as well. Think about it. If you immediately answer the demand for a lower price, haven't you shown the buyer that she does have more power than you? So this technique (buying yourself some time to think about the issue and calling the buyer back) not only allows you to think about the deal, but it also equalizes the buyer's power move. Try it. You'll like that feeling of equal power with the buyer!

Tactic #5: The Red Herring

The term *red herring* comes to us from the sport of foxhunting. Since foxhunting is really an excuse to party, and the party comes to an end when the hounds corner the fox, it didn't take the royal gamekeepers long to figure out that they needed a way to keep the dogs off the scent of the fox for a while so everyone would have a good time. Their solution was to drag fish (herring has a strong scent) across the game trails before the hunt started. When the dogs ran into the strong fish smell in the woods, it disoriented them and threw them off track. This stretched out the party back at the castle and kept everyone (except perhaps the fox) happy.

In the business environment, a red herring typically looks like this:

You sit down with a client to discuss your proposal, and he says, "Remember the problem that we had two years ago when you were late delivering the supplies to the Phoenix plant? That cost us two shifts of production. We figure we lost about fifty grand because of that. You are going to make us whole on this deal, right?"

The key here is the two years. If your client brings up some problem from the past in an attempt to get a price concession from you on a current deal, it is probably a red herring. If the old problem was really important to him, he wouldn't have waited two years to be compensated for it.

A red herring is used in one of two ways. It is an attempt to dredge up something from the past and beat you over the head with it in order to leverage a better price on today's deal, or it can be used as a delaying tactic to get the other side to agree to something you want just as long as they don't have to give you the red herring issue. Your customer may ask for something that they know you can't or won't give them. After peppering you with requests or demands that they know you will have to refuse (these are the red herrings), they offer to stop requesting whatever it is IF you will give them something else (what they really wanted all along). You are supposed to either feel guilty enough to make concessions or relieved that you don't have to give the client what he has been asking for all along.

Countertactic

Your best bet here is to acknowledge the issue, whatever it was, and then set it aside. You can say something like: "Yes, I remember when it happened, and it seems to me that there were some problems on both sides of that deal. If you would like, we can revisit it. However, that one doesn't have anything to do with the proposal we are here to discuss today. Let's get this one done, and then, if you like, we can go over the Phoenix situation and decide what to do about it."

To deflect this tactic when it is an old issue, you must separate the red herring from your current proposal. If the issue truly is a red herring, it will probably fade away on its own. Sometimes, you will actually have to deal with the issue. In either case, however, you will be far better off to look at it independently.

When it is used as a delaying tactic, you use the same set-aside technique, but do it early in the process to prevent long delays. There are hundreds of examples of red herrings used as decoys in international negotiations. Probably one of the most famous was the peace talks that occurred at the end of the Vietnam War. The North Vietnamese insisted that the shape of the negotiating table be circular so all the parties (including the Vietcong) involved would be seen as "equal" participants. The South Vietnamese wanted a rectangular table because a rectangle could show two distinct sides to the conflict, the North and the South. Eventually a compromise was reached in which representatives of the North and the South would sit at a circular table, with members representing all other parties sitting at individual square tables around them. Many scholars believe that the North Vietnamese were the instigators of these famous debates over the shape of the table, but actually South Vietnamese Prime Minister Nguyen Cao Ky wanted to drag out the debates until after the U.S. elections because he disagreed with then President Johnson's insistence that the Vietcong sit at the negotiating table as equals. Arguing over the shape of the table was a convenient way for the South Vietnamese to achieve their real end (delay) by focusing on a relatively small and unimportant aspect to the negotiation.

In a sales situation, a buyer might insist that his company get a three-year warrranty on your product, even though it is not an industry standard to do so. No matter what you say or do, he will not budge off his demand. In desperation, you offer another 5 percent off the already discounted price to close the deal. The buyer quickly relinquishes his three-year warranty demand and takes the 5 percent discount. If that sounds like a familiar story, you have experienced the wrong end of a red herring!

Tactic #6: Higher Authority

This is a classic tactic, and our friends the car dealers are masters of it. In practice, it usually looks like this:

You are working on an agreement with the buyer. Everything is going along great, some give-and-take on both sides, and eventually you shake hands on the deal. You sit back in your chair and start to relax, and she says something like, "This looks good. Now I just have to run it by the big guy."

Huh? What big guy? You thought that the buyer had the authority to do this deal. What are the odds that she is going to tell you that the guy behind the curtain loves it?

Zero.

This tactic is designed to give the buyer one more whack at the deal after you have put what you thought was your best offer on the table. The buyer is going to let you stew for a while and then come back and say, "Bob says we are very close. Knock off another 3 percent and you've got yourself a deal."

What are you going to do now?

Countertactic

The best way to deal with this tactic is to head it off up front. Early on in the process, you want to find out who the ultimate decision maker is. It is usually not polite to ask, "Do you have the authority to do this deal?" But it is perfectly acceptable to ask something like this: "Sarah, who besides you will be involved in this decision?"

If Sarah tells you that Jane and Bob need to sign off on it, then you certainly want to have them at the table when you get ready for final negotiations. You should never put your best deal on the table in the absence of the key decision makers. If they can't join the meeting for some reason, hold something back for the inevitable demand from them at the end.

For instance, you might be prepared to offer them ninety-day notice on price increases or dedicated inventory at your location. These concessions may cost your company very little, but they can be great "counternibbles" if the hidden "higher authority" demands more concessions.

Sometimes buyers don't play fair. One might tell you up front that he can do the deal and then try to surprise you with the higher-authority gambit at the end. You need to do your homework here. If you find out from other suppliers or from your own history with this company that the buyer is likely to try something like this, you can be prepared for it.

For one thing, you can hold something back. For another, when the buyer springs the tactic on you, it's fair to request that Jane and Bob (or the necessary people) join the meeting. You can say, "In order to save time and cut the potential for confusion here, why don't we bring them in so that we can get this wrapped up without a lot of back-and-forth conversations?"

Or you might ask to accompany the buyer when he takes your proposal to "the big guy."

The main issue here is that you don't want to cool your heels in a conference room while the buyer and his boss discuss the latest reality

TV show. Find out who the final authority is, and insist that the person (or persons) negotiate with you on a face-to-face basis.

Here is a real-life example:

We mentioned our friends the car dealers as effective practitioners of this tactic. They will leave you sitting in a little cubicle for twenty minutes or so while your salesperson and the sales manager pretend to talk about your deal. What they are really talking about is baseball, the weather, or the weekend boating trip. It only takes a minute or two for the sales manager to look at the deal and decide what to do.

In addition to the benefits of the higher-authority tactic (the salesperson isn't the one who wouldn't accept your offer; she is still "working hard for you"), there is another angle for the car dealer. They know that the longer you sit there and the more time you have invested in the deal, the less likely you are to walk out and start the whole process over somewhere else.

Here's how to handle this tactic. When the salesperson stands up to take your offer in, ask her to have the sales manager join you, or ask to accompany her to the sales manager's office.

If the salesperson says that the sales manager is too busy, write your phone number on the offer sheet, and stand up. Look the salesperson in the eye, and say, "Have him call me when he isn't too busy." And head for the door.

We can almost guarantee you that you will be in front of the sales manager within five minutes.

The higher-authority tactic is so effective because it creates an illusion that the party you are dealing with is collaborative and empathetic. It's the person behind the curtain who's being such a jerk. Don't fall for it! Find out up front who the person is you will really be dealing with, and get that person to the table.

Tactic #7: Split the Difference

All of you C4's pay close attention, because you are especially vulnerable here. This tactic is seductive because it seems so fair and reasonable: "Let's just split the difference and get out of here." There are several potential problems with this approach, and you need to be on the lookout for all of them:

- The spread is too big. If the difference between what you are asking and what the buyer is willing to pay is too great, you risk giving away too much by meeting in the middle. Remember, it is your margin that you are losing.
- The stakes are too high. You can't compromise on some things; company policy, legal issues, safety issues, and moral issues are areas where compromise can get you into trouble.
- It's a trap. Let's say that your asking price is $10,000, and the buyer wants to pay $8,000. After some back-and-forth conversation, the buyer says, "Look, this isn't getting us anywhere. Why don't we just split the difference and move on?"

Seems reasonable, doesn't it? Let's say that you agree. In the first place, a $9,000, you just gave up 10 percent of the gross on the deal and a much larger percentage of your company's margin. What's worse, if you are not careful, you will find yourself discussing other issues involved in the transaction. Before long, you might get stuck on another issue. At this point, the buyer looks up and says, "I've got other things to do today. I can't spend any more time on this deal. We're pretty close. Why don't we just split the difference and get on with our lives?"

What's going on here? If you aren't careful, you are going to lower your price from $9,000 to $8,500. How far have you come down? $1,500. How far has the buyer come up? $500. Do you have a deal? Not yet. Who is winning here?

Countertactic

We don't like splitting the difference as a negotiating tool. If you have the time, there is almost always a better alternative. The problem with this approach is that both parties (particularly the seller!) have to give up something, and someone is bound to feel that she gave up too much or didn't get enough.

We recommend that you respond to a buyer request to split the difference by saying something like this: "We could do that, but I'm not sure that would be the best solution for either of us. Why don't we keep working on this and see if we can come up with an answer that is a win-win for both of us?"

Okay, you say, but sometimes you really do run out of time and you've got to close the deal. Is it okay to split the difference then?

Yes and no. You still can't compromise on the legal, ethical, and company policy stuff, or you will get into hot water. You may have to split the difference in order to make the deal happen, but try to do so only under the following conditions:

1. The spread is relatively small, and the negotiated outcome is acceptable to your company.
2. You split the difference only one time.
3. Splitting the difference is conditional on closing the deal. You say, "If I'm able to do that, could we sign this deal now?"

Again, we discourage the use of splitting the difference in negotiations, but if you have to use it, be sure that your eyes are wide open.

Don't be lulled into a false sense of complacency just because it seems so collaborative.

Tactic #8: The Flinch

This tactic is the essence of simplicity, and, at heart, it is a fake nonverbal. It looks like this:

You have been asked to submit a proposal for a piece of business. On the appointed day, you show up and sit down with the buyer to discuss the deal. You take the proposal out of your briefcase and slide it across to the buyer, who picks it up, flips to the last page, looks at your price, and lets out a groan. He may even sink down in his chair and cover his face with a hand. Yikes!

His actions and body language convey to you how deeply disappointed he is in your proposal. In fact, he is personally hurt by your price. As a trained sales professional, you sense that the relationship you have so carefully cultivated is in jeopardy. You need to act fast to get things back on track. Right?

Wrong! You are being played. The purpose of these theatrics is to get you to do something rash. Let's think about what's really happening here. The buyer has asked for a proposal, and you have provided one. It's business. Your price may or may not have been in line with expectations, but it is not likely that any price would cause the buyer personal pain. Some buyers could be nominated for Academy Awards for their outstanding performance in a business situation.

Countertactic

Like the tactic itself, the countertactic to the flinch is incredibly simple. Since the reality is that you haven't hurt the buyer, there is no need for you to do anything.

That's right; just sit there and wait for the buyer to say something.

Unfortunately too many salespeople have a problem with conversational lulls. They want to jump in and say something or do something to repair the relationship. This is exactly the wrong thing to do, since it will generally involve giving something away in hopes of making up. If you simply sit there and wait him out, sooner or later he will figure out that you are not going to take the bait. Then he will start talking about your proposal, and you can get on with the negotiation.

Buyers know that salespeople are trained to nurture and maintain personal relationships with them. If they can convince the salesperson that the relationship is in jeopardy because of something in the proposal, they know that the salesperson might well start making concessions in order to heal the rift.

Ignore the flinch. Sit quietly, maintain eye contact, and let the buyer go first.

Tactic #9: The False Impasse

With this tactic, after a period of negotiation, the buyer looks at you and says, "Forget it. This deal just isn't going to happen. You might as well go home." She may even stand up to signal that the meeting is over.

It is often difficult to know whether you are truly deadlocked or whether this is just a tactic to scare you into doing something that you shouldn't. In most cases, you will have some sense of whether you were actually making progress. When things grind unexpectedly to a halt, you are probably looking at the false impasse. The message to you, the salesperson, is meant to be very clear: you are going to lose this deal!

Countertactic

Whether the impasse is real or false, you need to do something—and fast. Just don't react too quickly and think that suddenly dropping your price is the solution. Here are some things that you can do without getting into trouble:

+ Take a break. Sometimes a fifteen-minute break will completely change the atmosphere and dynamics of a negotiation. When the parties sit back down to discuss the deal, much of the tension and frustration will have evaporated. Sometimes new alternatives will present themselves that weren't apparent before the break.

+ Change the venue. If you are in a conference room or an office, go down the hall and talk in the break room. Go out for lunch. Reschedule the meeting for a neutral location.

+ Use a T-chart. Show what issues have already been resolved and what issues remain. If the list of resolved issues outweighs the other list, you obviously have made progress.

+ Change the shape or scope of the deal. Perhaps the project can be done in phases that coincide with the client's budget-funding periods. Perhaps the scope can be scaled down to meet the client's needs and still not break the bank. Sometimes just one or two issues hold things up. If possible, pull them out and make them a part of some future negotiation.

+ Change the people. Sometimes one or more individuals at the table are being unreasonable. If the team leaders from both sides have a good working relationship, they might agree to remove anyone who has become an obstacle to putting the deal together.

+ Use a mediator. On big deals, it is often worthwhile to bring in a third-party arbiter to mediate any differences that are holding things up.

+ Make a concession. If something is important to the other party but relatively unimportant to you, you might concede on this point in order to get things moving. Remember to ask for something, even minor, in return.

Don't panic. If you do, you will likely do something that you will regret later. That's the whole point of this tactic. Stay calm, and let the other party know that you feel there is a solution to the problem and that you are convinced a win-win outcome is there.

Tactic #10: The Cherry Picker

At some time or another just about every salesperson falls for this one. Here's how it looks:

You have given a quote on an extensive array of products and/or services, and the buyer says to you, "Congratulations, we have selected your company to supply us with widgets for the Framingham project. Since the time you submitted your proposal, we have narrowed the scope of the project somewhat, and we will need only five hundred widgets for this phase as opposed to the thirty thousand that we originally thought we would need. We are looking forward to working with you."

Or maybe he says, "Your products will be going only into our A stores in Phase 1 of our implementation, so our usage levels will be roughly 25 percent of our original estimate."

Or maybe she says, "Our purchasing committee has decided to go with your company for products X, Y, and Z. We will be sourcing products A, B, C, and D from your competitor."

In other words, you quoted the deal based on a specific bundle of products, and the customer now wants to pay the bundled price for less merchandise.

It is amazing how many good salespeople agree to this kind of deal. They figure that it is better to walk away with something than to start complaining and possibly blow the whole deal. That's why this tactic is so effective.

Countertactic

Your response needs to be immediate. When the buyer tells you that the deal has changed, then you are completely within your rights to tell him or her that you will need to review your pricing based on the new scope. Your original quote was based on the initial specifications. If the buyer has changed the specifications, then you are under no obligation to honor your original quote.

Tactic #11: Doctor No

The strategy here is for the buyer to always reject the seller's first offer. The goal is to put the salesperson on the defensive and to immediately begin whittling down the price, no matter how reasonable it may be.

Countertactic

The classic defense is to go in with an artificially high price and let the buyer beat it down to where you wanted it in the first place. Doing this lets the buyer feel that he has won something for his company. A newer technique that is often equally effective and more productive is to take the time to look for collaborative ways to create a win-win. Consider this example:

Some years ago, Tom was running the office products division of a consumer products company. The buyer from one of the new warehouse club operations approached him. These clubs were creating enormous turmoil within established distribution channels, but their volume potential was too big for anyone to ignore.

The buyer wanted to stock only two SKUs out of the very broad product line. One of those items was a standard-sized vinyl chair mat. At that time, most of the mats were sold through a two-step distribution system: the manufacturer sold them to a wholesaler for about $25.00, the wholesaler sold them to a stationery supply store for about $35.00, and the stationer sold them to the end user for about $70.00. Included in the stationer's markup were delivery of the product, removal of the old mat, and a billing arrangement for the end user.

The warehouse club buyer wanted to purchase the mats for about $22.50 and sell them for $25.00 on a cash-and-carry basis. Clearly this pricing arrangement was going to create problems for the traditional distribution channels, but the buyer was adamant that he was going to market them this way, with or without Tom's company's product. Efforts to raise the retail price point were fruitless.

The selling price negotiations began at $25.00. This was the best wholesale price and specified purchases in full-pallet quantities. Since the buyer wanted to sell the product at that price, he immediately began looking for a better deal. Rather than beat the author up on price alone, however, he was surprisingly collaborative. The conversation went something like this:

> *Buyer:* If I were to buy in full-truckload quantities, wouldn't the economies of scale be worth another percentage point or two?
> *Tom:* Yes.

> *Buyer:* How about if I gave you a standing order for X num-

ber of truckloads per month so that your manufacturing people could make them whenever they wanted and have them ready to go? Wouldn't that be worth another point or two?

Tom: Yes.

And so on. By increasing the order size and otherwise making it easier to do business, the buyer was successful in lowering the price to within about $1.25 of where it needed to be. And then the negotiations stalled. The buyer had exhausted all of the opportunities to save money on the scheduling and production side, but rather than give up and accept the higher price point, he continued to probe.

Buyer: What are the cost components in a chair mat?

Tom: Pretty much what you would expect: cost of the resin, time on the extruder, some post-molding operations, cost of the box . . .

Buyer: What box?

Tom: Each chair mat goes in a large cardboard box. The boxes cost about $1.50 each.

Buyer: We don't need boxes.

Tom: These mats have sharp teeth on them. How will people get them out of your stores and back to their offices?
Buyer: At these prices, they will figure it out.

And they did! Notice that, in this example, the buyer and the seller were being creative and collaborative. The price concessions that Tom made were more than offset by the savings on the new packaging solution. Because together they sold a lot of chair mats, the solution was a win-win. The postscript is that this new distribution channel, plus the big-box office products stores such as Staples and Office Max, played havoc with the traditional channels. But that's a story for another day!

Tactic #12: Shoot for the Moon

This tactic might also be called "ask for the ridiculous." The idea is to ask for something that is patently absurd and force the salesperson to say no, which makes the salesperson feel defensive. It also gives the buyer plenty of room to look as if she is becoming more reasonable when, in fact, even a less-extreme demand is still unreasonable.

Countertactic

If the offer is not realistic, reversing the ridiculous is often effective. Turn it around 180 degrees, and show the other party how silly it is. Say something like, "Really, Bob, if you were in my shoes, how would you feel about an offer like that?" or "What do you suppose my boss would do to me if I went along with a deal like that?"

Let's say that a client wants to build an addition onto a factory but wants to pay only $50 per square foot for the work. If the going rate for a project of this kind is $120 per square foot, then the offer is clearly outside the realm of the reasonable.

Rather than try to debate the merits of a ridiculous offer, you can point out how unreasonable it is by saying, "C'mon, Bob. That would be like me asking you to sell me your $10,000 printing presses for $4,000. It isn't going to happen. Let's talk about what we can do."

If you expose the buyer's proposal as undoable, then you can move things in the direction of what is possible and realistic.

Tactic #13: Dumb and Dumber

Remember the old TV show *Columbo*? The police detective played by Peter Falk used a facade of simplemindedness to irritate his suspects to the point of confession, just to shut him up and make him go away. Quite often, buyers will pretend to be slow-witted in order to draw out the negotiations. They may "forget" concessions that they have made in earlier meetings. They may "misunderstand" things that they have or haven't agreed to. They may constantly repeat the same objections, even though you have dealt with them multiple times.

Unless you know for certain that your buyer is an idiot, it is a good idea to assume that he is a lot smarter than he wants you to think he is, and his ineptitude is an act designed to get you to underestimate him. If you become frustrated or angry over the slow pace of the proceedings or the constant repetition, you have fallen for the tactic. Salespeople are not known for high levels of patience, and smart buyers know that they can use this to their advantage.

Countertactic

We recommend one of two approaches to this tactic:

1. You can pretend that you are just as slow-witted until the buyer gets frustrated and gives up the ruse.

2. You can keep very detailed notes of each discussion and begin your meeting with a summary of what has been covered and what has been agreed to. For this to work, you need to break each negotiating point down into as small a piece as possible and get agreement or buy-in

on each piece before you move ahead. You must constantly ask questions such as, "Are we clear on that point?" Eventually the buyer will get so bored with this that she agrees to a faster pace, or, in the worst case, you continue with this strategy until you have your deal.

Summary on Tactics

Remember several things about tactics:

1. Buyers use them because they work. They are designed to knock you off balance and get you to do something that you wouldn't otherwise.

2. Just because buyers use tactics doesn't make them evil. Buyers have to perform, or they lose their jobs. Think of tactics the way you would think of plays in a football game. The team with the best understanding of the rules and the best execution of the game plan usually wins. That doesn't make the team members villains. Understanding tactics is a key skill in the game of negotiations.

3. Recognizing the tactic and knowing the appropriate countertactic are important, but preparation is critical. If you can anticipate the other party's moves in advance, you can plot out your responses in your own time and on your terms. If you wait until the last minute, you have to think through all of this on the fly, and that puts a lot of pressure on you. Preparation gives you power!

> **> PROFESSIONAL NEGOTIATING TIP**
>
> Good negotiators and good salespeople recognize and respond to buyer tactics in a way that negates the power of the tactic without creating face-saving issues for the other side or giving away the store.

CHAPTER 6

WHAT BUYERS ARE SAYING WHEN THEY AREN'T SPEAKING

PICTURE YOURSELF AT A CRUCIAL POINT IN A MULTIMILLION-dollar negotiation. The boardroom table has papers strewn everywhere; stale donuts and empty coffee mugs are lying around. You have just asked the buyer for a decision on a major aspect of the deal.

There is a pause.

The buyer, while looking down, takes off her glasses, chews absently on the earpiece, and rubs the side of her neck with her other hand.

What should you do?

Maybe you think she's sending you a sign to bunt or steal. Maybe you missed the signals altogether. Maybe you noticed them but didn't know what they meant or how you should react.

The fact of the matter is that she has just sent you some important information. If you misinterpret it or fail to respond properly, you will hurt your chances of getting a deal. Let's take a quick quiz on what you should do next:

(a) Do nothing.

(b) Interrupt her thought process and rephrase your question.

(c) Take off your glasses and look down as well.

(d) None of the above.

Pick (a) and you are probably going to hear the buyer say something like, "No, we aren't going to be able to make this happen."

Pick (c) and you will get no initial response for a moment, then you'll probably get turned down as well.

The correct answer is (b). You need to respond quickly to the two strong nonverbal signals that she is sending to you. By taking off her glasses and looking down, she is probably thinking about how to tell you no. The second clue, the buyer rubbing her neck at the same time she is looking down, indicates that your question was either off the mark or too direct.

These signals are telling you that the buyer is not convinced of the value of your project. Not only that, but she is not happy about something that you have said. If you insist on asking for a decision now, the odds are that you will be turned down.

You need to interrupt her thought process, before she gets to no. You need to rephrase or restate your sales pitch in a more palatable manner before you can move forward with your deal.

Wouldn't it be nice if we could just look across the table and read buyers' minds? We would know what they were thinking, what they were planning, and how they felt about our proposals. We would also know whether they were interested or bored. We'd know if they were telling us the truth or flat-out lying. Wouldn't that be great? We can't turn you into a mind reader, but we can give you insight into what's going on behind that stony glare.

In 1967, UCLA researcher Dr. Albert Mehrabian led a project to study how we communicate with one another. The researchers weren't surprised to learn that we relate to one another on a number of levels. They were shocked, however, to learn that in face-to-face conversation, words were not the most important medium of communication.

They found that when we exchange information with one another, the relative importance of the various means of communication looks like this:

WORDS:	7 PERCENT
TONE OF VOICE:	38 PERCENT
NONVERBALS:	55 PERCENT

That's right, well over half of what we "say" to one another is nonverbal. This explains why a face-to-face meeting is more effective than a phone call and why a phone call is better than a fax or an e-mail when it comes to really communicating with another person. At least in a phone call you can hear the other party's tone of voice.

In this chapter, we will discuss how to read some of the most common nonverbal cues that you are likely to see during a negotiation. These cues are important indicators of what is going on in the other party's mind. This information is especially useful because he doesn't know that he is giving it to you!

Before we get started, though, we need to insert a caveat: interpret all nonverbal gestures in context. Just as any individual word is meaningless when taken out of context, so too are nonverbal cues. Sometimes a scratch is just a scratch. Context is everything.

For example, at a workshop several years ago, a participant approached one of the authors as the class filed out for a break. She said, "Please don't misread my body language as negative. I'm really enjoying the class. It's just that I'm four months pregnant, and I think that I might throw up at any moment." Talk about understanding context!

You are looking for a reaction to something that someone says or is saying. It will usually be instantaneous.

We will now describe sixteen of the most common nonverbal cues that occur in negotiations. We will also recommend what you should do when you see them. For additional information on the origins and science of nonverbal signals, we recommend that you visit these sites: Center for Nonverbal Studies at Spokane, Washington; and Columbia University.

It is also worth noting that these particular nonverbals are universal. We conduct workshops all over the world and have found applicability across cultural and geographic boundaries.

Steepling

What it looks like in context:

You are speaking about your product or your proposal, and you look across the table and notice that the other person has his hands together in front of his chest and he is touching the fin-  gers of both hands together, making steeples. Sometimes he may be tapping his fingers together lightly. Sometimes he is still. It's a unisex gesture; both men and women steeple.

What it means:

This is a superiority gesture. Translated lit- erally, this nonverbal means, "I already know where you are going with this. In fact, I know more about this subject than you do, and I wish you would shut up and let me talk."

What to do:

Shut up. If you keep talking, the other party will just become bored and frustrated. He wants to say something, and he isn't really listening to you. As soon as you can, stop talking and say something like, "How do you feel about what we have covered so far?" or "What do you think about the project?" The sooner you get him involved in the conversation, the better.

You will see this nonverbal a lot when you are dealing with your superiors, specialists, or government officials. Pick up on it right away and let them talk.

The Neck Rub

What it looks like in context:

You will usually see this cue after you have made a strong statement about something or said something controversial. You will notice that immediately after the statement, the other party reaches up and rubs either the back or the side of the  neck. A man might put a finger or two under his collar, or just touch the side of his neck.

What it means:

Something about what you have been saying has made him uncomfortable. The phrase "hot under the collar" is derived from the physiological changes that we all experience when we feel threatened. He isn't happy with you right this minute, so now would be a terrible time to ask for a decision on anything. In fact, you have to fix whatever it is that you have done before you can move ahead with your proposal.

What to do:

You need to back off. You are coming on too strong, and the other party doesn't like it. There are several ways that you can do this. If you are leaning forward, you can sit back a little in your chair. You want to be as nonaggressive as possible at this moment. You can say, "Before you answer, let me rephrase what I just said." Then you soften your position or your statements to make them a little more palatable. To soften your position,

1. sit back a little.

2. interrupt them before they can respond.

3. rephrase and soften your original statement.

Hand to the Nose, Mouth, or Lower Face

What it looks like in context:

This signal occurs when the other party is doing the talking. Usually she is responding to a question or telling you how she feels about your pro-posal. As she is speaking, you notice that she touches the lower part of her face. She might touch her lips, nose, or chin. Sometimes she will put her fingers over her mouth and actually speak through them.

What it means:

Danger! Danger! It is critical that you pick up on this signal because something isn't right here. This gesture tells you that the speaker is unsure about what she is saying, is lying to you, or is not confident about what she is saying.

At this point you don't know which is happening, but in any case, it means that the information you are getting from this person is suspect. This nonverbal is a carryover from our childhoods. Watch a small child try to hide her face when you ask her if she did something wrong ("No,

I didn't break my brother's toy!"). Kids are afraid that we will read their minds and catch them in a lie. Adults are cagier than that, but they will still unconsciously put a hand to their faces when they are nervous or insecure about what they are saying.

What to do:

Ask questions and try to figure out what's going on. For instance, if the buyer has just told you that he can get your products for less somewhere else, you might want to ask questions about what she is comparing your offer to. It's probably not apples to apples.

You don't want to make any kind of a decision or commitment based on the information that this person is giving you because there is probably something wrong with the data. Probe for more information.

Chewing on Glasses

What it looks like in context:

You will generally see this signal when you have asked for an opinion about your products, services, or proposal. You notice that the other party has taken off his glasses and is chewing absently on the earpiece or perhaps dangling them from one hand.

What it means:

The buyer has listened to what you said and is thinking about how it might work. This is a good sign because he is considering the what-ifs and trying to figure out if this makes sense for him.

What to do:

Nothing. Just sit there quietly and let him continue to mull things over. Salespeople generally hate a lull in the conversation and will jump in and start talking. This is absolutely the wrong thing to do at this point.

If you ask a person, particularly an analytical person, for an opinion on something and then don't give time for her to formulate the answer, you run a strong risk of annoying her. Wait for her to talk first!

Taking Glasses Off (Rapidly)

What it looks like in context:

You can't miss this sign! It will typically occur when you are at a difficult point in the negotiation or you have surprised the buyer in some way. He reacts by taking off his glasses and dropping them (sometimes slamming them) on the table. Then he may give you a fixed, steely glare.

What it means:

You can probably guess. Something you said has frustrated or angered him to the point that he is ready to go off. Yikes!

What to do:

Jump in and say something before he articulates whatever he is thinking. First, shift back in your chair slightly so that your posture is less likely to be perceived as aggressive. Next, say something like, "Before you answer that, let me rephrase what I just said." Then, soften or modify whatever you said to set him off in the first place.

You don't want to ask for an opinion or a decision, because you aren't going to like what he has to say.

Stroking the Chin and Looking Up

What it looks like in context:

You will see this cue when you ask the buyer for an opinion on whatever it is that you have been discussing. She will typically lean back, look up, and absently stroke her chin or touch the lower part of her face while looking up.

What it means:

It means, "I'm interested. I'm thinking about it. And I'm thinking about how it might work." This is a very good sign, but you need to be careful with your response.

What to do:

Nothing. Just sit there and let her think.

Wait for her to talk first. If you blurt something out just to fill the conversational void, you will interrupt her train of thought and probably irritate her. Wait her out and let her come to whatever conclusion she is heading for, because it will probably be a good one.

Stroking the Chin and Looking Down

What it looks like in context:

It looks just like the last cue, except this time the person is looking down.

What it means:

It means exactly the opposite of stroking the chin and looking up. He is not impressed, and he is probably thinking of a way to say no. These two similar nonverbal gestures are

vastly different in what they mean to you, and it is critical that you pick up on them and react accordingly.

What to do:

In this case, you don't want him to finish his thought process. You want to jump in and interrupt him before he tells you why he doesn't want to do your deal. You can say something like, "Before you answer that, let me give you a few more reasons why this program has been so successful elsewhere."

The key here is to pick up on the negative nonverbal and react quickly. Now is not the time to try to close, because you haven't made the sale yet.

Hand Supporting Head

What it looks like in context:

You are talking about your product or program, and you look across the table and notice that the buyer is resting his chin in the palm of one hand and supporting his elbow with the other. Is this good or bad?

What it means:

It means exactly what it looks like. He is really bored by whatever you are saying. He probably isn't listening, and if you continue to drone on, you are just wasting everyone's time.

What to do:

You had better get him involved—and fast. Stop talking and say, "Why don't you give me your thoughts on what we have covered so far?" If you don't do something to engage the buyer in the conversation, you aren't getting anywhere.

Hand to Side of Face with Finger Up

What it looks like in context:

In this case, you are talking, and you notice that the buyer is resting her chin on her thumb with the index finger pointing up toward the temple. Even though this gesture looks similar to the last one, it has a completely different meaning.

What it means:

She is listening. She is involved in your presentation. She wants to know more.

What to do:

Keep going. You are on a roll. Notice how close this nonverbal is to the previous example and yet how different its meaning.

This is why good negotiators train themselves to always be alert to body language. Remember, the buyers aren't aware that they are giving you this information!

Arms Folded across the Chest

What it looks like in context.

You know what it looks like. The buyer is sitting back in his chair with his arms folded across his chest.

What it means:

We all know about this cue, right? It means that the person is close-minded or not buying your ideas. Maybe. Maybe he is just cold. Maybe that is a comfortable posture for him. Remember our caveat at the beginning of this chapter: any nonverbal is meaningless when taken out of context.

If the buyer has been sitting that way since the meeting began, it may be just a habit for him. Let's assume, however, that he has been sitting with his hands in front of him on the table. You say something like,

"Wouldn't you agree that this is the best deal on the market right now?" At this point, he leans back in the chair and crosses his arms. Now you can assume that you have a problem. It's the reaction that is significant, not the posture in and of itself.

What to do:

You haven't made the sale, so don't ask for the order. Rather, you need to ask some questions about how the buyer feels about what you have covered so far. You need to identify and address his specific areas of concern before you move forward in the sales process.

Hand on Upper Chest or Pledge of Allegiance

What it looks like in context:

You will see this cue when he is talking. As he speaks, he puts one hand on his chest and rests it there or gently pats himself.

What it means:

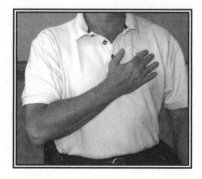

It means that whatever he is saying is a deeply held belief and it is important to him. Now, it might not necessarily be true. For instance, he could be saying, "Quality is the number one concern of this company." You happen to think that quality isn't even in their top ten. However, it would appear that the speaker believes it to be true and cares a lot about this issue.

What to do:

Make a mental note that the speaker feels deeply about this subject. You wouldn't want to challenge him on it unless you had a really compelling reason. It can also be a clue that this issue is or could become a face-saving one.

Head Rub

What it looks like in context:

You make a statement about your products, services, or proposal, and if you are talking with a man, you see him immediately put his hand to the back of his head. Men tend to smooth the hair on the back of the head. Women are more likely to touch their hair near the side of the face or brush their hair back behind the ears.

What it means:

Literally translated it means, "I can't believe you said that!" The buyer is shocked by or disagrees strongly with something you have just said.

What to do:

You need to rephrase or restate whatever it is in a way that is less likely to offend. There is no point in trying to move ahead with the negotiation until you fix whatever damage you have caused. You may need to ask general and open-ended questions to figure out specifically what the buyer believes may be the problem.

Hands Behind Head

What it looks like in context:

Although most nonverbals are gender-neutral, this one is almost exclusively male. You and the buyer are seated, and as you get into your presentation, you notice the buyer lean back in his chair with his hands locked behind his head. His legs are out in front of him, sometimes propped up on the table or an open drawer. You might see this in internal negotiations with your boss.

What it means:

Remember steepling? This is the same message. The guy's body language is saying to you, "I know a lot more about this subject than you do, and I wish that you would shut up and let me talk." It is a superiority pose.

What to do:

Stop talking and let him talk. Ask a question and then just sit back and listen for a while. Until you let him say whatever is on his mind, he isn't going to pay much attention to what you are saying.

The Starting Position

What it looks like in context:

This is another male gesture. You will generally see this cue after the meeting has been going on for a while. As you are speaking, you notice that the buyer has piled all of his notes into a neat stack and shifted in his chair. He is now facing toward the door and leaning forward. If you could see under the table, you'd see that his legs are bent in a position that resembles a runner in the starting blocks.

What it means:

Not good, is it? He is just waiting for you to take a breath, and he is out of there. In fact, he has already checked out mentally and isn't listening to whatever you are saying. He's bored and/or would much rather be somewhere else.

What to do:

You've got only two choices here, because he's not listening to you:

1. Try to reengage him in the conversation. Say something like, "How do you feel about the material that we have covered so far?" or "What's your reaction to this approach?" Sometimes this works, sometimes it doesn't, but you don't have anything to lose by asking.

2. Let him go. Wrap up the meeting, and try to get a commitment to resume at a later date.

The worst thing to do is to ignore the signal and keep talking. All you will do is frustrate the buyer and waste everyone's time.

Ear Tug

What it looks like in context:

You will generally see this gesture when you are well into your proposal. As you are speaking, you look across the table and notice that the buyer is tugging gently at his earlobe or rubbing a finger behind the ear.

What it means:

You need to quickly pick up on this non-verbal. A literal translation might be, "I'm interested in what you are saying, but I need more detail in order to really understand how it might work." It's a good sign, but you need to change your focus.

What to do:

Provide more details. Say, "You know, we've been discussing this project at a fairly high level. Why don't I give you a couple of examples of how it would work on a day-to-day basis?" Let him ask you about the specifics of your proposal, and make his comfortable that he is clear about the nuts and bolts.

Lint Picking

What it looks like in context:

You are talking about your program, products, or services, and you notice that the buyer is looking down and idly picking lint or something off the sleeve of her jacket.

What it means:

You are boring her silly! She isn't listening or interested in whatever you are talking about, and you are wasting everyone's time.

What to do:

Stop talking, and try to engage her in the subject with a question. If she still doesn't seem interested, give it up and come back another day with another strategy, because this one isn't working.

Summary

Nonverbals are as close to mind reading as most of us are likely to get. As we have seen in this chapter, your clients are giving you a lot of information through body language, but they don't know that they are sending it to you. Skilled negotiators watch for and read these signals very carefully. If you are negotiating as a team, you might want to designate one team member to just look out for nonverbals.

Here are final thoughts on this subject:

1. Remember to look for context. Sometimes a scratch is just a scratch.

2. Practice, practice, practice. Make it a point to look for nonverbals

at cocktail parties, sporting events, conventions, or anywhere you can observe people without hearing what they are saying. Try to infer what's going on by the body language. Airports and hotel lobbies are great training grounds for observing people as well.

3. Confirm the nonverbal message by asking questions.

Look for changes. Even if you can't remember what the gesture means, a change can signal acceptance or rejection of your ideas.

CHAPTER 7

THE GENDER DIFFERENCE: IS IT REAL?

MUCH HAS CHANGED IN THE WORKPLACE SINCE 1970. Dramatic increases in the number of working women combined with legislation preventing gender-based discrimination have led to a significant narrowing in the traditional gap between men's and women's wages. Recently, however, progress has slowed. As of the year 2000, women earned just over $0.73 for every $1.00 that men earned, and that number was up only marginally (1.6 percent) from 1990.

Certainly lingering sexual bias and the good old boy network are still partially to blame for this discrepancy, but recent studies have shown that there are far more complex factors at work as well.

In their groundbreaking book on the subject, *Women Don't Ask*, authors Linda Babcock and Sara Laschever uncover and document a number of cultural, sociological, and behavioral factors that also appear to affect the progress of women in the business world. Many of their findings are particularly pertinent to women engaged in selling because, more often than not, sales compensation plans are directly tied to success in negotiations (sales).

Here are some of their more significant points:

Women Don't Ask

As the title of their book suggests, the authors found that women were much less likely than men to ask for things (promotions, raises, concessions, a better deal, etc.). Numerous factors lead to this reluctance, but the net effect is that women often end up with less in business dealings simply because they don't know or are reluctant to ask for more.

Failure to negotiate effectively for oneself in salary discussions, for example, can have catastrophic effects over one's working life. The authors calculate that a $5,000 salary differential in an entry-level professional position (when compared to a male candidate, who is much more likely to negotiate a higher starting salary for himself) can result in an earnings deficit of about $500,000 projected over the course of a career.

They conducted a poll of graduating master's degree candidates at Carnegie Mellon and found that 57 percent of the male students negotiated the salary offers that they received from their prospective employers. Only 7 percent of the women did the same. In both cases, the students who negotiated were offered starting salaries averaging $4,000 more than those who didn't.

Here is a real-life example:

One of our female colleagues accepted a mid-level managerial job several years ago with a large financial services company. The terms of the offer were attractive, and the job requirements were a good fit for her. The company had also hired a male manager with the same job description at the same time.

Since they started on the same day and went through the orientation process together, it was only natural for them to compare notes on their backgrounds. Their educational and work histories were remarkably similar.

Imagine our colleague's surprise when she found out that her coworker had started out a full salary grade above her despite having the same job description. In addition to a number of substantial perks, her friend's starting salary was $10,000 higher!

When she asked how he managed to get such a good deal, his reply was simple. He said, "I just asked around and found out how the comp system worked and asked to come in at a level X. At first, they balked, but eventually they said okay and that was that."

Our colleague was shocked and angry when she found this out, but she was mostly disappointed with herself. It had never occurred to her that the pay package might be negotiable. The offer was in the ballpark of what she was looking for, so she took it.

It was an expensive lesson for her, but she vowed never again to accept any kind of a salary offer at face value. The issue isn't that she got outnegotiated. It's even more serious than that. She never even knew that she was in a negotiation. She didn't know that it was okay to ask.

Clearly the stakes are large and the incentives are high when it comes to salary negotiations, promotion opportunities, and other business-related discussions, but many women tend to see such negotiations as a conflict that may damage their relationship with the other party. Seen in this light, they will often avoid the conflict by settling early or taking what is offered.

Men, on the other hand, are more likely to see a negotiation as a sport or a game with rules and procedures. They may actually look forward to negotiation as a way of testing their skill level against the other party's.

Given this radically different mind-set, it is not surprising that women are less likely than men to ask for things and to initiate negotiations.

These same studies have shown that women, much more so than men, are reluctant to blow their own horns. They would much rather that their coworkers and managers notice and reward their hard work and dedication than to have to bring up those traits themselves.

While modesty is an admirable trait, it is a fact of life that in business you typically end up with what you can negotiate for yourself rather than what you deserve.

What You Need vs. What You Deserve

Research shows that in basically identical situations, women tend to place a lower value on their work than men do. Men will typically benchmark their earnings goals on what other men are making or what they think they should be making. Their salaries become an indicator of success and progress compared to their peers'.

Women are more likely to think of salary considerations in terms of what they need. This tends to make women less focused on salary growth and more tuned in to other aspects of their jobs as far as their overall satisfaction levels at work.

Obviously most companies are not going to force more money on employees who aren't asking for it. This reticence in salary negotiations can, as we pointed out, have serious ramifications over the course of one's business career. Likewise, the failure to sell or negotiate aggressively for the company can have an equally grim impact on one's prospects for promotion.

Gender Norms and Stereotypes

Society expects women to behave in a certain way. We typically do not expect women to negotiate forcefully and aggressively. Women who do so run the risk of a significant backlash.

Behavior that would be tolerated or even admired in a man can create all sorts of image problems for a woman. A guy who pounds the table, yells, and bullies may not be loved but, quite often, earns grudging respect or even admiration (think Donald Trump). A woman who engages in identical behavior (think Martha Stewart) won't be so lucky. Such a woman is almost certain to be demeaned and ridiculed by her male and female coworkers alike.

By violating society's expectations for how a woman "should" act, the aggressive female can create all kinds of problems for herself. The B word is always lurking in the background, and it is the rare organization indeed that puts such a person on the management fast track.

It is a small wonder then that most women shy away from the kind of confrontational, in-your-face negotiating style that gets men labeled as hard chargers. This also helps to explain why car dealers will routinely quote higher prices to female customers than they do to males for the identical vehicle.

It's not fair, but whoever said life was going to be?

Negotiating with the Other Sex

Negotiations are complicated enough when men negotiate with men and women with other women. When you cross gender lines in negotiations, things can really get messy. Men, in particular, seem to have a problem negotiating with women on an equal basis.

Many men will fall into one of two camps when it comes to dealing with women. The C1 (conquer) types will tend to see women as potentially weak and therefore exploitable. They will try to bully their way to a better deal. They might get loud, pound the table, or stand and try to physically intimidate their female counterparts in order to further their ends.

Other men will go to the opposite extreme. They are so afraid they are going to hurt a woman's feelings or be perceived as hostile that they deliberately tone themselves down to the point that they become almost timid.

Neither style, of course, is particularly productive. For negotiations to be truly satisfying for both sides, there must be an atmosphere of mutual respect and trust so that information can be shared, options can be considered, and alternatives can be discussed.

What to Do If You Are a Woman

Seek professional negotiations training from a reputable source. Once you begin to view negotiations as a discipline with clearly defined rules and skill sets, you can begin to approach negotiations with more confidence. By learning how to play the game, you are much more likely to negotiate effectively for yourself and your company without becoming emotional or strident and without pushing those pesky gender norms.

Women are also more naturally collaborative than men. As you will remember from our discussion of styles (Chapter 2), the collaborative negotiating style is an excellent fit for many (but not all) business situations. Woman can use this style to make their negotiations more productive and satisfying for all parties concerned.

Since women are generally more emotional than men, they need to use the techniques described in this book to remain calm and professional during their negotiations. Any sign of emotion will be perceived as weakness.

The bottom line is that there are differences in the way that most men and women approach negotiations. In the business world, these differences are likely to work against women.

Yet, despite these differences, women can be just as effective as (or more so than) their male counterparts. Women, like men, can benefit from negotiations training, and they can use what they learn to their advantage. In fact, because society's expectations are fairly low for women in this regard, women have the element of surprise on their side.

For a more in-depth look at the research on the differences between men and women when it comes to negotiations, we highly recommend *Women Don't Ask* by Linda Babcock and Sara Laschever.

CHAPTER 8

THE LOST ART OF
SAVING FACE

SEVERAL YEARS AGO OUR FIRM WAS BROUGHT IN TO MEDI-
ate the breakup of a small consulting business. The two partners (let's
call them Pat and Fred) had decided to go their separate ways. They met
at their offices on a Saturday morning to try to divide up the assets of
the company. We were there to facilitate things in the event that they
deadlocked over any issue.

First, they split up the client list. Doing this might have been a
problem, but they had decided to break up the business by product
line and the clients fell into each of the product categories without any
overlap.

Next, they split up the liquid assets of the company. There was
about $200,000 in cash on hand, so each partner agreed to take half.

Then, they dealt with such issues as employees, leases and contracts,
and so forth. Everything proceeded smoothly and in a very predictable

manner. Even the items that they anticipated would be problematic were handled efficiently.

With the major issues out of the way, they turned to the subject of the office furniture. It was several years old and had an appraised market value of about $30,000. To everyone's surprise, Pat leaned across the table and said to Fred, "I get all of the furniture. You get nothing."

His astonished partner, Fred, said, "Over my dead body!" and the negotiations came to a screeching halt.

Our colleague suggested a fifteen-minute break and took Pat outside. He tried to uncover the issue behind his position but couldn't get him to divulge his reasons.

Our colleague then met with Fred and told him that the furniture was nonnegotiable. They discussed options for a while, and finally he said, "I'll take $175,000 of the cash, and he can keep the furniture and the remaining $25,000."

When he pointed out that this was neither fair nor reasonable, Fred simply said, "Just take him the offer."

To our surprise, Pat immediately agreed and signed off on the change. The rest of the assets were divided without incident.

As the parties were packing up after the meeting, our colleague asked Pat why he was willing to pay such a high price for the furniture. He declined to give his reasons.

Several weeks later our colleague happened to run into him and asked him again why he had made such a big deal over the furniture.

Here's what Pat told him: "We started that business many years ago on a shoestring. It was just the two of us and our spouses. We worked together, socialized together, vacationed together. As the years passed, we grew apart, and somewhere along the way, our wives developed a dislike for each other. As I was getting ready to leave for the meeting on that Saturday morning, the last thing my wife said to me on the way out the door was, 'I picked all of that furniture out. It's ours. Don't come home without it.'"

Pat did what he had to do to save face with his spouse.

The point of this story is not to explore the internal dynamics of this guy's marriage. Rather, we want to give you a real-world example of how face-saving issues can pop up suddenly and stop a negotiation in its tracks. If you aren't aware and on the lookout for this possibility, you can make things much more difficult than they need to be.

We teach negotiation skills all over the world, and in most cases, the skill sets and tactics are universal. Face-saving is an interesting exception to the norm because although it is important everywhere, many Western cultures tend to ignore face-saving as a negotiation skill. This is a big mistake. Most Eastern cultures are far more sophisticated in terms of recognizing and dealing with face-saving issues as they arise. Since understanding the importance of face-saving is such a critical skill, this chapter will address the importance and impact of face-saving in negotiations.

Face-saving issues aren't usually obvious and may not be directly connected to the business issues under discussion, but they are as real and as important as anything else being negotiated.

> ➤ PROFESSIONAL NEGOTIATING TIP
>
> There is usually at least one face-saving issue in every negotiation. Being able to recognize a face-saving issue can be critical to your success.

What Kinds of Things Create Face-Saving Situations?

Face-saving situations can be caused by any number of things going on behind the scenes. Some of the more common causes are these:

+ Someone is new. Anytime you have a person who is new to the company, you have the potential for face-saving issues. A new person almost always feels that he needs to validate the hiring decision by performing well in the negotiation. If the new person's boss is in the room, he will feel particularly pressured to do well. If the new person is the boss, he will feel that he needs to demonstrate his capabilities to the employees. Whenever you enter a negotiation and find out that someone on the other side is new, either to the position or to the company, you should immediately be on the lookout for face-saving issues.

+ The other party has overcommitted. Sometimes the other person does something stupid. Maybe she tells you that she has the authority to do a deal, and then she finds out that she does not. Maybe she has told the boss that she can buy your products for 40 percent off list price, but you can't go past 25 percent. Maybe all of her projects are over budget and behind schedule. Maybe her job is on the line. These are her problems, right? Wrong! They are your problems too. Unless you can figure out a way to make her look good, you don't have much chance of getting your deal done.

+ Something is going on higher up. Maybe your buyer hasn't done anything dumb after all, but maybe her boss has. Maybe the company committed to the financial community that it was going to increase sales by 15 percent and profits by 20 percent this year. If it's July and both sales and earnings are flat, I can guarantee you that the face-saving problems at the "C" level are trickling down to every department in the company. There are probably memos flying around every week about the need to cut costs, boost sales, tighten belts, and so forth, and you had better believe that such an atmosphere will affect your negotiations.

These are just examples of things that could create face-saving situations for your clients. You can certainly think of others. Again, the point is that they are just as real to the other party as any other issue on the table, and sometimes much more important.

As you prepare for your negotiations with a customer, you should always be aware of the things that might create face-saving issues. If you can uncover them up front, you can put together a strategy to deal with them, just as you plan your pricing moves and your fallback positions (Chapter 9).

Your insight into another organization will never be perfect, however, and sometimes you are going to be blindsided by a face-saving issue that you didn't anticipate. To deal with it effectively, you must first figure out what's going on.

Several things might tip you off that someone is trying to save face, but the number one indicator is this: you are in the middle of a negotiation and things have been proceeding more or less the way you thought they would. All of a sudden, the other party digs in his heels and starts behaving in a way that doesn't make sense to you. That's when the little light should go on in your head that says, *Uh-oh. We've got a face-saving problem here.*

Recognizing a face-saving situation is half the battle, sometimes the hardest half. Okay, now that you have recognized it, what are you going to do about it?

> ➤ PROFESSIONAL NEGOTIATING TIP
>
> A sudden change in behavior during a negotiation can be a signal that the other person may be in a face-saving situation.

+ Confirm your suspicions. And how do you do that? By asking questions. You might say something like, "Help me understand why this particular point is so important to you," or "Tell me a little bit more about why you feel so strongly about this." Try to get your client to tell you what the face-saving issue is. Sometimes he will come right out and say it. At other times you will have to guess or infer it from what he will (and won't) tell you. In either event, you must determine what your client needs in order to save face. Only then can you start thinking about what to do.

+ Figure out how to help solve the issue. If you are ever going to take the negotiation to the next phase, you are going to have to figure out how to make it look like the buyer got what he needed. If it's a price concession, you must come up with something that looks like a reduced price. (Notice that we didn't say you had to cut your price. We said that you needed something that "looked like" a price cut. You can change the scope or timing of the order to change the shape of the money if that will make the buyer look good.) If the problem is terms, delivery dates, warranty, or training, you need to work very hard to get what the buyer needs. Otherwise, he will dig into his position, and the only thing changing will be the level of frustration in the room.

+ Figure out what to ask for in return. Once you have a good idea of what the other party needs in order to save face on her end, you need to figure out something of at least equal value or greater to ask for in return. (Remember, in negotiations, we never give something away without asking for something back.) If you can identify the face-saving issues up front, then you can work up your list of things to ask for in advance. If the face-saving issue pops up unexpectedly, then you might have to come up with something on the fly. It's a good idea to put together a list of things you might want to ask for just in case you run into this situation. Examples might be a longer term of contract, more units of existing items, more SKUs from your company's product line offering, or quicker payment terms.

> **➤ PROFESSIONAL NEGOTIATING TIP**
>
> In order to resolve face-saving situations, figure out how to give the other party what they need in order to save face and then figure out what you are going to ask for in return.

You get the idea. Just because the buyer has a problem is no reason for you to have to give away the store. To reiterate, you've got to come up with a way to get the buyer what she needs and then make sure that you get something of equal value or greater for your company in return.

Let's say that you are calling on the new purchasing manager for a major potential client. In planning for the call, does it make sense to go in with your lowest price as an opener? No, purchasing people are usually evaluated on their ability to negotiate lower prices from suppliers. You need to open with an offer that has some room in it. In order for your buyer to feel that he "won," he needs to be able to show his superiors that he did a good job for them. As you let him negotiate on price, you should have some things that you ask for in return for the concessions.

Lest you think that face-saving is confined to the kinds of situations we've described to this point, think about some of these that have come up in our workshops:

Real estate transactions. Imagine the dynamics between a residential Realtor and two sets of spouses (buyers and sellers). Quite often the real fireworks aren't between the buyers and the sellers but between the spouses over things such as pricing strategies, accepting or rejecting offers, and so on.

Investments. The spouse in charge of managing the money has blown most of it on dot-com investments. He or she has done this over the objections of the couple's financial adviser. The three of them sit down to review the damage to the portfolio. Any face-saving issues here?

Price quotes. A salesperson has let a customer beat her up to the point that she agrees to an outrageously low price. Upon reviewing the deal, the sales manager rejects it as unacceptably low. What is the salesperson (or the sales manager) going to do now?

Delivery times. In order to match a competitive offer, a salesperson quotes an eight-week lead time on an item that can't be produced in less than twelve weeks. The salesperson's attempts to move the project to the front of the queue don't work. Who is going to call the customer with the bad news?

Not all face-saving situations are played out on such small stages. Perhaps you remember this one from the news accounts:

On April 1, 2001, a U.S. Navy EP-3E surveillance plane was disabled in a midair collision with a Chinese F-8 fighter plane. The Chinese aircraft plunged into the South China Sea, and neither the plane nor the pilot was ever found.

The U.S. plane lost its nose and one of its four propellers in the incident. The pilot, Shane Osborn, made an emergency landing on China's Hainan Island. The plane was immediately surrounded by Chinese soldiers, and its crew of twenty-four was detained.

China and the United States blamed each other for the incident.

China demanded an apology from the United States as a condition for the release of the crew. The Chinese were also adamant that the spy plane would not be allowed to fly out of Chinese airspace, and that all surveillance flights in the area cease.

For its part, the United States denied causing the incident, which it blamed on a "hotdogging" Chinese pilot, and demanded the return of the crew and the plane.

Over the next several days, each side dug into its position, with the public statements ratcheting up in intensity.

The Chinese said the U.S. plane would "never fly out of Chinese airspace." They also began asking for reparations of $50 million (U.S. dollars) to compensate them for the loss of their fighter plane and its pilot. They wanted an apology for causing the incident and for landing the damaged plane on Chinese soil without permission.

For its part, the United States was still demanding the immediate release of the crew and return of the plane.

These escalating tensions were threatening what had been a growing tone of cooperation between the two countries on a variety of important matters. Behind the scenes, negotiators for both sides were working around the clock to defuse the rhetoric and find a way to resolve the dispute with no loss of face for either side.

Finally a breakthrough was achieved on April 11. Here's what happened:

+ President Bush issued a statement expressing "sorrow for the loss of the Chinese pilot" and for landing our plane in Chinese territory without permission.
+ The United States chartered a civilian plane to bring the navy crew home.
+ The spy plane was dismantled and shipped out inside a giant Russian cargo plane.

+ The United States paid China something less than $50,000 (U.S. dollars) for expenses related to the incident.

So how were the face-saving issues resolved?
For the United States:

+ The Americans never directly apologized or accepted responsibility for the incident.
+ They didn't pay anywhere near the $50 million (U.S. dollars) in reparations.
+ They got the crew and the plane back.
+ They did not agree to stop surveillance flights.

For China:

+ The Chinese got a statement from President Bush that sounded a lot like an apology when translated into Chinese.
+ They got to say that the United States compensated them for the incident.
+ The U.S. plane did not fly out of Chinese airspace under its own power.
+ They did not admit to any responsibility for the incident.

In the end, both sides got what they needed in order to save face with their own people and the international community. This allowed them to get back to the business of negotiating vital trade and economic deals with each other. This potentially explosive situation was resolved by negotiators who understood the importance of saving face.

The ability to recognize and deal with face-saving situations is one of the key differentiators between great negotiators and everyone else. Now that you have learned what to look for and how to react in these situations, you might be surprised at how much more effective you can be when things get tough.

We Can Create Our Own Face-Saving Situations

Another point to consider: Although other people or events can certainly create face-saving problems for us, our own egos are just as often to blame.

During a coffee break at a recent workshop, a very successful businessperson told a face-saving story of his own to one of the authors. Here's what he said:

> A couple of years ago, we put our house on the market, and it sold almost immediately for the full asking price. The buyers expressed an interest in a large, handmade swing set that we had built for our children. The swing set did not convey with the other property, and they made us an offer to buy it.
>
> Since our children had long since outgrown swing sets, I was interested in selling it, but the offer was, in my opinion, way too low. I had put a lot of thought and effort into building it, and I wasn't about to let it go at a bargain-basement price.
>
> The buyer wouldn't come anywhere near what I thought the thing was worth, and we both dug in our heels.
>
> Eventually we both gave up on reaching any kind of a deal. I ended up paying someone to dismantle the thing and haul it to the dump. All because I was too stubborn to accept a low price. Not the greatest business decision that I ever made, but at least I understand now why I did it.

A representative from one of our Fortune 500 clients called us recently to say he needed help in negotiating an agreement that involved splitting up a payment that the firm had committed to a client. Our first question was, "Have you thought about the face-saving issues around this request?" The silence on the other end of the phone was all we needed to hear. Even though it turned out to be a reasonable request based on circumstances, the fact that the client had to save face internally had to be dealt with or the contact was never going to hear the request.

Understanding and responding to these situations can be the difference between getting your deal and beating your head against a brick wall.

One more example, and this one is also from a workshop with Vistage (formerly known as TEC). A participant told this story:

I had a long-standing agreement to buy out the founder of our company after ten years. When the time came to actually put the buy-out agreement together, he balked. I knew that he wanted to get away from the aggravation of running the business, but he dug in his heels and refused to discuss selling out.

It took me three months to figure out what was going on. His problem with selling was that it would leave him either (a) unemployed or (b) retired. He didn't want to be either of those things. He didn't want to have to tell his buddies and his cronies at the club that he didn't have a job.

Once I figured out what the problem was, it didn't take long to come up with a solution. We created a new title for him, vice chairman. This gave him something for his ego, and it gave me what I wanted, control of the company. If I hadn't figured this thing out, I don't think that he would have ever sold me the business.

Again, there is usually at least one face-saving issue in every negotiation. Don't enter into a negotiation without figuring out what that issue might be, and don't forget to look for other face-saving issues as you negotiate. If the other party suddenly stops being reasonable and digs in on a particular point, don't keep pounding away on that point and expect that he will miraculously change his mind and start acting rationally. You've got to ask enough good, open-ended questions to figure out what's going on, what he needs in order to save face, and perhaps most important, what you are going to ask for in return in order to help him put this problem behind him.

As they say, "Try it. You'll like the results!"

Examples of open-ended questions/probes to uncover face-saving issues:

+ Help me understand why this particular point is so important to you.
+ What has changed at your end since the last time that we discussed this deal?
+ I don't understand why we are having such a hard time with this issue; can you help me see it from your perspective?
+ Could you give me some more background information on how we got to this point?
+ Is there something going on behind the scenes that I need to know about in order to move this deal along?
+ I get the sense that I might be missing something here; can you help me get a better picture of where we are?

CHAPTER 9

PLANNING:
THE KEY TO POWER

A FEW YEARS AGO, RON WAS ASKED TO HELP PREPARE A
Virginia company for a negotiation with a large utility in the Northeast.
Our client had done work for the utility, and after the work was completed, the utility had decided that the amount of the change orders was
too great and too expensive. The author went to the client site and for
two days made two vice presidents and the president prepare and then
practice a twenty-five-minute opening again and again until they had it
nearly perfect. The president then called the utility and asked if they
could open the meeting scheduled for two days later. The utility agreed.

Two days later the meeting began at the utility site. After the three
representatives of our client presented their nearly flawless opening, the
senior vice president for the utility slammed his fist on the table, and
dead silence followed. As they waited for his "explosion," he turned to
his team and said, "These people are well prepared for this meeting, and

we are not!" Then turning back to the team from our client, he said, "I apologize for my team not being prepared to address your opening comments. We are going next door, and we will be back in about an hour." With that, the utility team left the room.

Over the next four hours, our client got virtually everything the team asked for in their opening comments! Is planning effective? We think so.

We can almost hear what you are thinking, though, *Wow! Planning, I'll bet this is going to be an exciting chapter!* Maybe yes and maybe no.

It all depends on how you define exciting. The fact of the matter is that effective planning is the key to having power in negotiations. We have made that statement several times so far in this book, and we will probably say it again before we are finished. By thinking through what you are going to do and how you are going to do it, you can prepare yourself for the objections, the tactics, and the roadblocks that the buyer will undoubtedly throw your way. All of us would like to have more power in our negotiations, and planning is the surest way to get it.

Why Planning Is Important

Preparation allows you to develop your strategy calmly and logically as opposed to "on the fly" in the meeting itself. Done properly, planning will give you power in several important ways:

+ It removes the pressure you feel when you have to ad-lib a response.
+ By thinking through what the other party is likely to want out of the negotiation, you can anticipate the strategies and tactics that the other party is likely to use. You can then create effective counterstrategies and countertactics.
+ By looking at the issues from the perspective of both parties, you

can identify areas of common interest and use them as a basis for collaboration.

✦ You can think about potential face-saving issues and how you might handle them.

✦ You can separate the issues that are going to be relatively easy to deal with from the really tough ones. Then you can look for solutions to both.

✦ You can make a list of nibbles and/or counternibbles (see Chapter 5) and have them handy when it is time to make trade-offs.

✦ If you identify your "walkaway" point in advance, you remove the possibility that you will get emotionally involved in the negotiation and do something unwise.

✦ You can think through what you are going to do if, for some reason, this deal doesn't happen. Knowing in advance what you will do if this negotiation fails will keep you from getting panicked into doing a bad deal.

So, if the idea of walking into a tough negotiation with a well-thought-out action plan under your arm is appealing to you, maybe this chapter will be exciting after all.

The Process

Lots of salespeople think that they are already planning. By "planning," they are referring to the ten minutes they spent in the vendor waiting area and the notes that they scribbled on the back of a company brochure. Maybe they called their sales manager and talked about the account for a few minutes the day before the call.

This isn't planning. This is a recipe for getting your pocket picked.

Our company is involved in many complex negotiations, and we realized years ago that planning was going to be essential to our survival and success. None of the canned approaches worked for us, so we developed our own. Over the years, we have improved and refined this template. You will find a copy titled, appropriately enough, "Negotiation Planning Worksheet" in Appendix I of this book.

This is a deceptively simple document. We have printed hundreds of thousands of copies and distributed them to workshop participants all over the world. Many of them have installed the form on their hard drives and modified it to fit the particular negotiating scenarios they encounter regularly. That's fine with us. These same clients also report savings of almost $2 billion and counting as a result of using this tool, so there must be some value in it. Let's walk through it and see how it works:

What They Want

We always start with this issue. Why? Because if you know where the other party is coming from, you can develop a strategy to deal with her. Empathy, the ability to put yourself in someone else's shoes, is a critical skill for an effective salesperson and a great negotiator.

Another reason to start here is that this is often the most difficult part of the process, and it is best to tackle it when you are fresh.

So what does the other party want? Don't oversimplify here. Really think through it. Of course, she wants low price and acceptable quality, but what else is important? Here are some examples:

+ on-time deliveries
+ logistical support
+ accurate billing statements
+ advertising support
+ R&D help on new products

+ special packaging
+ dedicated inventory
+ custom colors/sizes
+ low return rate
+ consolidation of suppliers
+ long-term relationships

And so on. It is extremely useful at this point to make this list as comprehensive as you can for the particular customer that you are preparing to meet. The more knowledgeable you are about her concerns, the better prepared you will be when you develop your strategy.

> ## ▶ PROFESSIONAL NEGOTIATING TIP
>
> Empathy, the ability to put yourself in someone else's shoes, is a critical skill for an effective salesperson and a great negotiator.

What I (We) Want

Once you have completed the customer's wish list, you need to think through what you hope to take away from this negotiation. Again, be thorough. You want to get (at least) a fair price for your products or services, but what else do you want out of the deal? Consider these examples:

+ a satisfied customer who will refer additional business to you
+ low return rate
+ on-time deliveries
+ a closer working relationship on new products under development
+ no invoicing headaches

+ opportunity to sell additional items to this customer
+ purchasing schedule to facilitate better manufacturing efficiencies for your company

The point here is that there is usually more involved than just price and quantity, and you need to think through what the other issues are so that you can use them in developing your strategy for this account. They will also help to ensure that you have a strong value proposition.

Possible Matches

After you have finished both lists, you need to go back and compare them side by side. You are looking for matches, that is, instances where you and your customer desire the same thing from the negotiation. For example, both might have "low product returns" on your lists. Both probably want things to run smoothly on the paperwork side with a minimum of bookkeeping problems. Both want the quality of the product delivered to meet or exceed expectations. And so on.

This step gives you a list of things with which you are in agreement with your customer. As you have already read in Chapter 4, you can begin your meeting with a nice collaborative opening statement like this:

> We have been looking forward to getting together with you this morning. In preparing for this meeting, we have tried to look at the issues from your side as well as our own. We have identified some areas where, we think, we are already in agreement. For example, we both have an interest in developing a long-term, mutually beneficial relationship. Both of us want to see this project succeed beyond its original budget. We have the opportunity here to develop some leading-edge technology that

will reflect well on both companies. There are some areas where we have some ideas on how to solve these issues in a way that we both win.

This may seem to be a small point, but by opening the meeting in this manner, you can accomplish several things, all of them good:

1. You are telling the other party that this meeting is important to you so you have prepared for it. You aren't going to fumble around and waste his time (like many of the other salespeople who call on him).

2. You are telling him that you have looked at things from his point of view. This means that you aren't totally focused on "winning" for your side.

3. You have found some areas of agreement in objectives. Every point is not going to be WWIII.

4. There may be some difficult discussions on some points, but you have looked for win-win scenarios as opposed to win-lose solutions.

If you do this properly, you will make your job a lot easier because the buyer may let down his guard a little bit if he thinks you aren't out to get him. When this happens, he is much more likely to share information with you and work toward truly collaborative solutions on the more difficult issues.

Key Areas of Discussion

This is just a nice way of saying, "What do we think the problem areas are going to be?" Maybe it's price. Maybe it's delivery dates. Maybe the buyer wants a size or a color that you don't offer. Maybe it's all of the above. Whatever you have identified as the tough issues needs to be thoroughly considered well in advance of the meeting.

You may need to brainstorm with other team members or colleagues to come up with innovative solutions. You need to look at all possible alternatives from the customer's point of view and see which ones do the best job of satisfying her business and personal agendas.

If you can come up with at least one creative, win-win solution to the items on this list, you are way ahead of someone walking into a meeting with an important customer and just hoping to come up with something that works.

Okay. So far, everything that you have written down on this side of the planning sheet is collaborative and empathetic. In fact, there is no reason why, in theory, you couldn't share this information with your customer. We stress *in theory* because you wouldn't actually do this, but if the buyer should accidentally get a look at the front page of your planning sheet, all she would see is that you have tried to look at things from her point of view as well as your own and that you have tried to identify the areas where you are likely to be in agreement and the areas where you've got work to do. Nothing wrong with any of that, is there? It reinforces the message that you are a hardworking professional and that you have prepared for this meeting.

Nevertheless, we don't recommend showing the buyer the sheet because you still have work to do on the back side, and you emphatically do not want her to see what you've got there.

Their Measurements

Knowing how your customer is measured will give you insights into how he is likely to behave during the meeting, what will be important to him, and where he is likely to dig in.

For example, let's say that your customer is a purchasing manager and his bonus is tied to his ability to negotiate discounts off list price. What are the odds of your success if you go in with a "list price or nothing" strategy? That person is going to need to show his management that he has done his job by getting a "better price" and a great deal for the company.

If your client has a special incentive to get a project wrapped up in eight weeks and you quote a twelve-week lead time for a critical component, what is the likelihood that you will be signing an order?

A client recently related an interesting story to us that reinforces this point:

> My company does a lot of business with a particular branch of the government. I had a lot of problems with my buyer until I figured out that he was being measured on how closely our proposal and the final invoice corresponded. As long as those two documents were basically identical, he looked good to his boss and was, therefore, a happy camper. Price wasn't the issue at all!

See why this information is so important?

There are any number of ways to identify these measurements, but the best way often is to ask the other party straight-out, "What do you need from this discussion to show your management that you have done a good job for them?" Other sources for this information would be other salespeople, coworkers, company reports, trade associations, ex-employees, and so forth.

You need to figure out, in advance, where the other party is coming from and what she needs in order to look good. If you can figure out how to give that to her, the negotiation is going to have a better end result and will probably "go down" a lot easier.

Face-Saving Issues

What is going on with this buyer and/or this company that might create face-saving issues for them? Think through this point carefully. Here are questions to ponder in regard to face-saving issues:

+ Is the buyer (or his boss) new to the job or to the company?
+ Is the buyer's job secure, or is she in trouble?
+ Is this project on time and on budget?
+ Is the buyer's company in good financial health?
+ What are stock analysts saying about the company?
+ Who else will be sitting in on the negotiation?
+ Does the buyer really have the authority to do this deal?
+ Has this person made a statement or "drawn a line in the sand"?

You can use the same sources that you used for your other information to help you try to answer these sorts of questions. The key is to identify, up front, what these issues might be so that you can formulate a strategy to allow the buyer to save face while not giving away anything that you don't want to. You also want to think through what you'll ask for in return.

Unless you create a solution, your negotiation is going to be more difficult because the buyer isn't going to agree to a proposal that makes him look bad. Find a way to make him a hero. Just be sure that you know what you want in return.

Pricing Moves

Having to make concessions during a negotiation is fairly common. As painful as it is to give something up, it's a lot less painful if you have thought through, in advance, how and when you might concede on something. For the purposes of this discussion, we will focus on pricing moves, but the same rules and strategies apply to nonmonetary concessions such as payment terms, length of contract, scope of work, or whatever.

Walkaway Price

Always begin with the walkaway price. Why? Unless you already know at what point you are no longer interested in a deal, you might get carried away by emotion and do something you will regret later. You always want to put in writing the number you won't or can't go below.

To illustrate this point, let's create a fictitious deal. The numbers don't matter; just follow the thought process:

In preparation for a negotiation with an important client, you go over the numbers for a deal and decide, based on your costs and company guidelines, that if you can't get the deal for $13,500 or more, then you don't want the business. So $13,500 becomes your walkaway price.

By determining what this number is and writing it down, you have removed the possibility that you will make a major pricing blunder in the heat of the moment. This knowledge gives you confidence, which leads to power.

> ➤ PROFESSIONAL NEGOTIATING TIP
>
> Always know your walkaway price and write it down.

Maximum

This is the best price that you could hope to get out of the deal. In some cases, it will equate to list price. In others, it will be an ideal price based on cost plus a high gross profit for your company. In any event, the maximum is what you would get if everything went perfectly and the buyer behaved the way that you would like him to behave. Let's call it about $15,000 for the purposes of this example.

Which leads us to our next point: never quote a deal like this with a round number. Round numbers look made up, and they invite negotiation. Anyone can figure what a 5 percent or 10 percent discount is from that number, and believe us, he will. On the other hand, a number like $15,286 looks as if you stayed up all night building a zero-based price. So you will call this your maximum.

> ➤ **PROFESSIONAL NEGOTIATING TIP**
>
> Try to avoid round numbers in your quotes. Round numbers look made up, and they invite negotiation.

Starting Point

This is the number that you will use when you open the negotiation. In some cases, it will be your maximum; in others, you may decide to start with a lower price because of your customer's buying power, an existing business relationship, or competitive market pressures. If you are calling on a purchasing agent for a large company, the odds of your getting out the door with an order at list price are exceedingly slim—even if you have a unique product or service that the customer needs and can't get anywhere else. You need to allow a buyer to feel that she has "won" and gotten some concessions for her company. Otherwise you risk putting her in a face-saving situation with her peers. Even if you have the power to do that, she will never forget that situation, and she will look for a way to get even with you.

So, you need to think through your starting point. It has to be realistic, and you need to be able to support your number if asked. It shouldn't appear to be made up or inflated.

Let's say that you decide you're prepared to offer the package that the customer wants for $14,665. That's your starting point, and it's almost 5 percent off your list price. Notice that it isn't exactly 5 percent. Again, it looks like there is logic at work here that is based on the cost components involved. You aren't just knocking fluff out of the deal.

First Move

So now you have a maximum price. You know that you are going to go in and show this particular customer a price, which, based on market pressures and the customer's volume (and professional pride), makes sense. It is our sincere wish that by using the skill sets and techniques in this book, you are able to shake hands and walk out with an order at this price. But what if you can't?

What if the buyer acts like a buyer and threatens and kicks and screams? You need to be prepared to make a pricing move if necessary. The time to figure out what this move should be is not while sitting in the buyer's office. You need to consider and plan for this possibility in advance.

We recommend three things at this point:

1. Don't discount in even numbers. Use 3.7 percent rather than 4 percent, for example, because it looks like there is much more thought and analysis in your number!
2. Continue to avoid round numbers.
3. Ask for something in return!

Remember, a good negotiator—and you are a good negotiator—never gives up something without asking for something in return. As soon as you figure out what a 3.7 percent discount on $14,665 is ($542), you write the new net price ($14,123) in the "First Move" section (see Appendix I).

Now, before the ink is dry on that price, you need to drop down to the box "Additional Items" (counternibbles) and list the things that you are going to ask for in return for the discount. Typically you might ask for these things:

+ a larger down payment
+ quicker payment terms
+ additional items under contract
+ longer contract terms
+ consideration for future business

Some of these things may not be of great value to you or your company, but it is important for your client to understand that your pricing is fair and based on logic and that if you are going to modify your price, you will need something in return from her.

> **PROFESSIONAL NEGOTIATING TIP**

If you lower your price without asking for something in return, you just told your customer that you were trying to take advantage of him!

Second Move

In some negotiations, the deal will get done at this point. In others, it will drag out through multiple iterations. It is a good idea to be prepared to make at least one more move. All of the rules for the first move apply here plus one more. And it is a biggie. Your second move must always be smaller than your first move. Why? Because if your second move is larger, you are sending a message to the other side that there is a lot more room in the deal, and they will come after you like pit bulls.

In this example, your first move was 3.7 percent. If you have to make a second move, we recommend that it be around one-half the magnitude of the first move. Let's call it 1.8 percent, or $254. Remember, this is your gross margin that you are giving away, so you want to drop down immediately again to the "Additional Items" section and list a few more counternibbles that you will ask for if you need to make this move. You are now at $13,869 on your price, and you are getting close to your walkaway price.

You can plan on additional moves if you think that you might need them. The point of all this is that each move should send a silent message to the buyer that you are getting closer and closer to your "I haven't got another dime" point.

Don't get hung up in these numbers. The strategy is what is important. Let's recap:

+ Don't use round numbers for your quote.
+ Don't discount in even percentages.
+ Make pricing moves progressively smaller in terms of dollars and percents.
+ Always ask for something back when you have to give up something.
+ Plan all of the things in advance and write them down.
+ Always have your walkaway point written down.

> **PROFESSIONAL NEGOTIATING TIP**

Each succeeding pricing move must be smaller than the one previous to it.

Additional Items (Counternibbles)

We have already listed several counternibbles earlier in this chapter and touched on how to use them. As you think about the following counternibbles, think of things the buyer might give you that wouldn't cost him much but would be valuable to your company:

+ pricing guarantees
+ minimum order or usage guarantees
+ forecasts for your inventory planning
+ additional business in other categories
+ flexible production and/or shipping schedules
+ more favorable payment terms

Every industry and deal will be different, but you can probably identify some of these items that you can use again and again in the course of multiple negotiations. At the same time, you can prepare a list of things that are valuable to the clients and don't cost your company much. These might include the following:

+ nondisclosure agreements
+ extended warranties
+ training or technical assistance
+ dedicated inventories of finished goods
+ guaranteed delivery times
+ co-op ad monies

Think as much of this through as possible before you walk into the client's conference room. If you can anticipate and write down what you are going to ask for and what you are prepared to give up, you avoid much of the pressure and panic that occur in front of the client. You will be the one proceeding calmly and rationally. The client will be scrambling to figure out whether she is winning or losing.

Alternative Strategy

Last but certainly not least, you have to consider the possibility that this deal might not happen. Despite your best efforts, sometimes you just can't come to an agreement. If you haven't considered and planned for this possible outcome, a shrewd buyer will use an impasse to create additional pressure on you.

It is always useful to spend some time thinking about alternatives. This is not being negative or planning for failure. Quite the contrary. What you are doing is saying, "How will I accomplish my goals and meet my company's expectations if, for some reason, this particular buyer is unreasonable or one of my competitors does something crazy?"

You almost always have alternatives, and you need to write them down, for instance:

+ You can sell the same products to another client.
+ You can sell different products to this client.
+ You can develop a new client for this product.
+ You can sell to this client by going around the buyer and selling directly to the user(s).

Having alternatives gives you confidence that your future is not riding on this particular deal. You have other ways to reach your objectives if this one doesn't pan out. That knowledge prevents you from being panicked into doing something that you shouldn't do. Alternatives are the source of real power in negotiations.

Let's recap what the planning sheet for our fictitious deal would look like.

Negotiation Planning Worksheet

WHAT THEY WANT	WHAT WE WANT
High quality	Satisfied client
On-time delivery	Fair price
Low price	6-week lead time
No billing headaches	Commitment on purchase quantities
4-week lead time	
No minimum usage guarantee	More SKUs under contract
Consolidate vendors	Referrals to other clients

POSSIBLE MATCHES?

High quality / Satisfied client
Consolidate vendors / More SKUs under contract

KEY AREAS OF DISCUSSION:

Low price / Fair price
4-week lead time / 6-week lead time
No minimum usage guarantee / Commitment on purchase quantities

THEIR MEASUREMENTS?

Bill is measured on his ability to cut costs.
He also must meet standards on quality, delivery, and returns.

FACE-SAVING ISSUES?

Bill has a new boss. Also, last year he almost lost his job when a new vendor couldn't meet the shipping dates that he had promised. Bill's division had to shut down a line for two weeks while they waited for raw materials.

Maximum: $15,286

Starting Point: $14,665 (-4.1%)

First Move: $14,123 (-3.7%)

Second Move: $13,869 (-1.8%)

Minimum (walkaway): $13,500

ADDITIONAL ITEMS (COUNTERNIBBLES):

Additional SKUs under contract

Larger down payment (30% vs. 20%)

Quicker payment terms (15 days vs. 30 days)

Longer-term contract (24 months vs. 12 months)

ALTERNATIVE STRATEGY:

Sell a similar deal to XYZ Corp.

Sell Bill our "value" line instead of the higher-priced product we are quoting.

Get the operating divisions to spec our products.

Before we leave planning, let's discuss another idea that great planners should be aware of before they enter the negotiation room. Does the name ZOPA ring a bell? Probably not, but having a ZOPA is a critical piece of any planning session.

ZOPA is a funny name and an important topic. A ZOPA is typically needed in order to get to a deal in a seller-buyer negotiation. So what's a ZOPA? Simply: zone of possible agreement.

Let's say that a salesperson has established a walkaway price of $100,000 and a target of $155,000. The buyer has a walkaway of $115,000 and a target of $80,000. There is a ZOPA in this agreement. In this illustration, the ZOPA is where the two ranges overlap: $15,000.

Had the buyer set a range between a low of $50,000 and a high of $80,000, there would be no ZOPA. Obviously the higher the amount in the ZOPA, the more the likelihood of reaching an agreement exists.

How can salespeople use this information? The best way to build a ZOPA is in the planning phase. Often, you can estimate what you think the other party is willing or likely to do. Asking questions in the actual discussions will help to confirm that a ZOPA exists. ZOPA can also be determined by looking at market pricing, this customer's purchasing history, your past experience in giving concessions, and so on.

As we discussed, salespeople should always have an alternative solution in any negotiations. The strength of that alternative solution will affect the ZOPA equation. If you have a strong alternative strategy, you may want to share part or all of it with the other side. If the other party's alternatives are weak or nonexistent, she may well decide to modify her ZOPA in order to reach a deal. If the situation is reversed, as it often is for the selling side, and you cannot get the buyers to change their walkaway or scope, you may conclude that no ZOPA exists, and then you are the one to break off the negotiations rather than invest more time and energy in a lost cause.

So, based on your planning, here's what you know:

+ What you think you are going to be talking about
+ What you will probably agree on
+ What issues might present problems
+ How the buyer is measured (his motivation)
+ The face-saving issues that you might see or hear
+ What you will do if you have to make a pricing move
+ What you will ask for in return if you have to make those moves
+ What you will do if the deal doesn't happen
+ Whether or not there is a zone of possible agreement

Now, isn't that a lot more than you usually have figured out before you walk into a meeting? When you look across the table and see that the person on the other side has a blank legal pad in front of him, you know that you are prepared and he isn't. Guess what? You've got the power!

No one can anticipate everything that will come up in a negotiation. There will always be a curveball or two that will come your way. Yet, if you can prepare yourself for 70 percent or 80 percent of the issues and obstacles that you are likely to face, your odds of doing well go way up. That is what this process is designed to do.

The first time that you go through this exercise, it might take you forty-five minutes. The second time, you can do it in thirty minutes. Before long, it is a fifteen- to twenty-minute process. Isn't it worth fifteen or twenty minutes of your life to be able to avoid the panic and pressure of an ad hoc negotiation?

The more important the negotiation, the more important the planning process becomes. Our rule on this is simple:

If you haven't planned, don't go. Period.

> PROFESSIONAL NEGOTIATING TIP

If you can prepare yourself for 70 percent or 80 percent of the issues and obstacles that you are likely to face, your odds of doing well go way up.

CHAPTER 10

NEGOTIATION STRATEGY

THE BUYER FOR A LARGE MANUFACTURER WANTED A BETTER discount on the specialty chemicals he was ordering from a supplier. Try as he might, the supplier would not budge from his price. At the beginning of a new quarter, the buyer decided to start ordering smaller shipments (just enough to get by on) and kept delaying the larger orders for inventory. The worried supplier began calling the buyer and looking for his "regular" orders. No deal. One week before the end of the quarter, the supplier (now way below his year-to-date projections) called the buyer and tried again for a large order. The buyer agreed to a large order but only if he got the discount that he had been seeking. The supplier reluctantly caved in to the demand.

Our buyer had successfully used a timing strategy to get what he wanted. The seller once again "took a lickin'." By the way, we hope you noticed the use of the red herring tactic. That's good because the tactic and this particular strategy go hand in hand.

Strategy is a word that is used often and just as often misunderstood. We find that the most common strategy in sales negotiations is: "We have to win this business—whatever it takes." Is it any wonder that the buyers do so well against us? Walking into a negotiation without a clear-cut and cohesive strategy is like using bows and arrows against a machine gun!

Why is a strategy so important? We think the Chinese general Sun Tzu summed it up best in 550 BC in his writings that were later collected into the book *The Art of War*. He wrote,

> In ancient times, those known as great warriors prevailed when it was easy to prevail. Their victories were not flukes, because they positioned themselves so that they would surely win, prevailing over those who had already lost. So it is said that great warriors take their stand on ground where they cannot lose. Therefore a victorious army first wins and then seeks battle; a defeated army first battles and then seeks victory.

Sun Tzu understood that planning before the battle decides the outcome. He knew that a good strategy takes into account what the enemy might do and creates a plan for multiple possibilities. Today, we call this a robust strategy.

Before you as a salesperson can develop a strategy, you have to assess the situation. We recommend the tried-and-true SWOT analysis. You start by taking a look at your Strengths and Weaknesses, your Opportunities and any Threats. Then you do exactly the same thing from the perspective of each of your competitors.

What types of strategies are out there, and which ones work best? Let's identify each type and examine how and when each is most effective:

Direct Strategy

This strategy is used infrequently in sales negotiation planning because in order to pull it off, you have to be incredibly strong or big or both. Only powerhouses like Wal-Mart, Microsoft, General Motors, the federal government, and some monopolies have the clout to pull it off. Practitioners of this strategy generally use conquer style in negotiations. As we have previously mentioned, this is not a good style to use if you have strong competitors. If you cannot use a direct strategy, then you will have to take an indirect approach. We have listed several of the most effective indirect strategies below.

Divide Strategy

While planning the negotiation, you realize that you cannot win the entire business. In fact, winning it all could lead to disaster in some cases. For example, winning the company's entire business might over tax your systems, but a piece of it now would get your foot in the door and allow you to build up your capacity enough to go after the whole thing later. Your strategy might be to appear to go for it all but compromise and get just a piece of the business (the piece you really wanted in the first place).

The divide strategy is a good one when your competitor already has the business sewn up. You decide that you can't overwhelm your opponent with brute force, so you select a segment of the business where you can offer a unique or quantitative difference, and you go for that portion. In sales negotiations, you often face these situations when you negotiate with people who won't or can't see the value you bring to the table. In these cases, you need to use a divide strategy in order to get in front of other stakeholders who can appreciate your value proposition.

Sometimes, in situations where you are blocked from seeing these critical stakeholders, you may have to use others (internal champions) to accomplish your goals.

A great example of this came to one of the authors through a friend, David Burns, now retired, who was a career trade negotiator for the U.S. government. In dealing with Taiwan, U.S. trade negotiators were stymied for years by the problem of pirated books, records, and other intellectual property. Copyrights had virtually no meaning in the Taiwanese culture, so illegally copying books, CDs, and movies became big business. For years, U.S. trade negotiators talked to politicians and professional negotiators who would put a little pressure on the Taiwanese judges for a short period of time. The judges would fine the perpetrators a token amount (usually around $50) and let them go. Using a divide strategy, U.S. trade negotiators went around the lawmakers and went directly to the Taiwanese judges and convinced them that they needed to impose stiffer sentences and much larger fines in order to stop these illegal activities. Eventually the strategy worked. The volume of pirated CDs dropped dramatically.

Timing Strategy

This strategy was used in our opening story of this chapter. If you have power and can take the business now, then try to engage the customer in early negotiations. You don't want your competitors or even your customer to gain strength by waiting. If you don't have a lot of power, maybe delaying some pieces of the negotiation will allow you to gain more strength during the wait period.

Timing strategy is used more often than you might think. For example, say you have lost a deal and your competitor is very tight with the buyer. You know that the buyer is going to retire in six months. Rather than bang away at the old buyer and risk creating a hostile atmosphere, the smart salesperson will begin laying the groundwork and building relationships with the team that will take over after the retirement. In any negotiations that come up during that time frame, the seller would be wise to try to delay any major negotiations until after the retirement of the unfriendly buyer.

Exploiting Strategy

After you do your SWOT analysis, you will know where you are strong and your opponent is weak. Once the negotiation begins, you will focus on concentrating your power against your opponent's soft spots. An example might help:

Let's say that your company is known for producing the highest quality products in your industry and your competition can't match your quality. In a negotiation with a large customer, the procurement person tries to get you to lower your price and threatens you with "the loss of a lot of business" to a competitor if you don't lower your price. If you know that this customer needs your level of quality, then you have the power to exploit your advantage and refuse to give in to the buyer's demand.

Perhaps your competitor has a no returns policy, and your company will take anything back. You exploit the competitor's no returns policy by constantly pointing out this discrepancy to potential purchasers of the product.

Let's take another global example to see how this strategy can play out on a big stage. Remember our friend Dave, the U.S. trade negotiator? Dave told one of us about the incredibly tough negotiations between the United States and Japan over the importation of U.S. automobiles into Japan. The Japanese took the position that American-made automobiles were inferior to Japanese products and, therefore, were not suitable for their market. A few token U.S. cars were imported and sold, but the balance of trade was wildly skewed in favor of the Japanese. Dave's team tried everything they could think of and got nowhere.

As a last resort, Dave's team said to representatives of Lexus, "When your cars come into port in San Diego, they must then be driven to the LAX airport for duty inspection. We are suspending the valuation" (which meant that each Lexus entered the country duty-free, but the United States could put any amount of duty it wanted on each car after the fact). The ships carrying brand-new Lexuses to San Diego turned around and went back to Japan.

The next step was a meeting in Geneva, Switzerland, with all concerned parties. At that point, Dave's team approached the Japanese with the idea of selling American-made parts rather than complete cars in Japan (you'll notice a bit of the divide strategy here too). Given the quid pro quo of resolving the Lexus duty problem, the Japanese agreed to the proposal, and billions of dollars in American-made tires, mufflers, roof racks, and other aftermarket products flowed into the Japanese market. The United States recognized that cars were a longer-term fix, so they exploited the strength of U.S. manufacturing (a wide variety of good aftermarket parts and accessories) and a weakness of the Japanese side (poorer quality and selection in the aftermarket), and made it happen.

A seller should look seriously at which strategies are likely to be most successful before entering into a negotiation with a buyer. If the seller's position is relatively weak, then perhaps they want to delay things until they are stronger. If the seller has a new innovation, how quickly can they get the negotiations over and the product to market? Any long delays in negotiating a deal could provide a competitor time to catch up.

Sellers should also think about where they are strongest and how they can leverage this strength for maximum impact.

Remember, no single strategy is right for every situation. If you do a good job on the SWOT analysis, you shouldn't have a problem coming up with the right plan for your particular situation.

CHAPTER 11

POWER: HOW TO GET IT AND HOW TO HANG ON TO IT WHEN THE ACTION GETS HEAVY

WE HAVE WRITTEN ABOUT POWER A LOT SO FAR, AND there's a good reason for that. Power in negotiations gives you leverage, confidence, alternatives, and control. These are all good things to have. We'll need to backtrack a bit in order to isolate the origins and dynamics of the power equation. The question is, What do you have to do to give yourself power, and, just as important, how are you going to hang on to it once the negotiations begin?

This last point is critical because power is fluid. Just because you have it now doesn't mean you will still have it later. Power moves around during a negotiation, and, if you are not careful, you can give it away without knowing it. Good negotiators know what to do to give themselves power before they ever sit down with a buyer. They also constantly monitor what's going on in order to track shifts in power. If they are losing it, there are steps that they need to take immediately to get it back.

Power is also largely perceptual. If you think that you have it, you probably do. If you think that you don't have it, you don't. But remember, just because you have it going into the negotiation doesn't mean that you necessarily get to keep it!

In this chapter, we will discuss how to get power, how to keep it, how to recognize tactics that the other party is using to grab your power, and what to do if you find yourself losing power.

Let's start off with a real-life example of the way power can shift (or, to be more precise, can be manipulated). We'll use our buddies the car dealers again because they are masters at this:

Let's say that you have decided it's time for a new car and you want to buy a Stratomatic 5000. When you think about the negotiation logically, who should have the power as you walk through the doors of the Stratomatic dealership?

You should because

+ you've got the money; you can decide to spend it or not.
+ you don't absolutely have to buy a car.
+ even if you did have to buy a car, you don't have to buy a Stratomatic.
+ even if you did have to buy a Stratomatic, you don't have to buy from this particular dealer.
+ you certainly don't have to buy a car today.
+ even if you have made up your mind to buy a car today from this particular dealer, you can go online and get all kinds of information, including dealer invoice, incentives, what other buyers are actually paying, and so forth.
+ when it comes to transportation, you have lots of options, and options give you power.

And yet how many of us feel powerful when we think about the car buying process? Not many. And why is that? Because long before you actually walk through the door of that dealership, the car guys have set up a series of gambits and traps that are designed to shift power away from you and back to them.

I'm sure that you have already recognized a lot of the tactics that we described in Chapter 5 as tools of the trade for car dealers:

+ higher authority
+ nibbles
+ split the difference
+ the bogey
+ time pressure

These and a few more are in their playbook; for example, in our area virtually all of the dealerships have signs on the wall stating, "All transactions are subject to a $299 processing fee." What is a processing fee except additional profit for the dealer? And yet people pay it because the sign says they have to. In our experience, dealers will drop the fee in a heartbeat if you challenge them on it, but most people simply shrug their shoulders and go along. After all, what can you do about it? It says right there in black and white that you have to pay it!

We don't mean to pick on car dealers (too much). They serve an important function, and they need to make a profit to survive. It's just that the system has evolved in such a way that, with a few exceptions, they have to manipulate their customers as much as possible in order to stay in business. Is it any wonder that most of us look forward to the car buying experience about as much as a trip to the dentist? Chapter 19 is devoted to taking the pain out of this process. But we are digressing.

Power: How to Get It

There are some obvious sources of power in a negotiation. Buyers for Wal-Mart or General Motors have tremendous purchasing power. Sales representatives for Microsoft have the enormous installed base of systems users to leverage. If you have an exclusive, patented idea that is red hot, you've got power.

For better or for worse, most of us don't get to deal from this kind of negotiating posture. As salespeople, we have plenty of competitors, our buyers can source product from all over the world, and they have been trained by pros on how to leverage their strengths with the tactics and methods that we have been discussing.

Nevertheless, there are things that you can do to give yourself power in these negotiations. First and foremost is preparation. Planning gives you power. If you were paying attention in Chapter 9, you know that planning allows you to plot your strategy, your pricing moves, and your tactics in the relative solitude of your office or a conference room rather than on the fly in front of your customer.

If you already know what you are going to do in several different scenarios, you don't feel the pressure that accompanies an ad-lib negotiation. Having established a walkaway position gives you power. If you know up front at what point you no longer want the business, you don't have to worry about getting manipulated or emotional and committing yourself and your company to a bad deal.

> ➤ PROFESSIONAL NEGOTIATING TIP
>
> The more you know about the customer, the better prepared you will be; and the more prepared you are, the more power you have!

Having alternatives gives you power. If you have already thought through what you will do in case this particular negotiation fails, you avoid the panic that might cause you to do something you might regret later on.

This power will translate into a sense of confidence that will allow you to conduct your negotiations calmly and professionally and will help you to stay unemotional when things get tough.

So we have established that power is good and that you want to get more of it. Besides planning, what else can you do to get power?

Know Your Customer

The more you know about the internal organization and business practices of your customer, the better you will be able to anticipate the tactics the buyer will use, the questions he will ask, and the things that will be important to him.

For starters, you would certainly want to know:

+ How is the overall health of the company?
+ What kinds of problems is it having that your products might address?
+ How does your particular buyer fit into the organizational structure?
+ Who else is going to be involved in the negotiation?
+ Do they have a history of using particular tactics again and again?
+ Is the buyer's word good, or does he play games?
+ Is this new business for you, or do you have a track record with the company?
+ Who's the competition?
+ What is the time frame for a decision on this deal?

Where do you go to get this information? The Internet and the company's Web site are good sources for the big picture. For the nitty-gritty details, you can turn to other (noncompetitive) salespeople who call on the account, or sales or customer service types in your company who have experience with them. Industry trade associations or informal networking organizations can sometimes be quite good sources of data.

At any rate, the more you know about the customer, the better prepared you will be with answers for whatever the customer throws at you.

Know Your Competitor

Rarely will you negotiate in a vacuum. There are almost always one or more competitors lurking in the background. Therefore, you need to know as much as possible about the strengths and weaknesses of each.

For example, if your primary competitor is a known price-cutter (aren't they all?), then you need to be prepared to counter the low price with service, features, reliability, or whatever. You should never be surprised or unprepared when the buyer brings up the competition. For each competitor, you should have a clear and compelling explanation for why your company and your products are the right choice.

When researching the competition, you should look for

+ *areas where you have a clear advantage.* If you have an advantage with features or price, great. If not product or price, maybe you are better logistically, or maybe you can provide better service internationally (see Chapter 10). Look for an advantage, and then see where your edge fits against your buyer's priority list. In other words, if you identify shorter lead time as an advantage and the buyer doesn't care, then you need to find another advantage.

+ *competitive weaknesses.* These might not show up in head-to-head product comparisons, but maybe they are weak financially, maybe they have legal problems, or maybe they have a history of over-promising and underdelivering. Negative selling is very risky, but you certainly need to know this stuff. Sometimes you can point the buyer in the right direction, and she will dig up the facts on her own.

Again, the Internet and your contacts in the industry will be your best sources of this information. Other competitors will often tell you a lot.

Know Your Company

You need to know the good, the bad, and the ugly about your company in order to formulate an effective strategy. Always try to look at your company from your customer's (and your competitors') point of view. Be realistic.

In addition,

+ think about how all of your product offerings may help in the negotiation. Sometimes you can justify a higher price based on a broader product selection.
+ look for areas where your company's other activities might help the buyer and his company achieve their goals. Maybe you have internal expertise that can help the customer solve an ongoing problem. Maybe you can help the customer break into a new market or can put the buyer in touch with another supplier for something that his company needs.
+ watch for opportunities to collaborate on future projects.
+ constantly seek ways to meet your client's needs through new product and process development. Alert your management to these opportunities as soon as you identify them.

Know Yourself

Before you leave your office, think about your negotiating style (see Chapter 2) and that of the buyer. How will you modify your natural tendencies in order to make the negotiation proceed more smoothly?

If you tend to become emotional or defensive, how will you monitor your behavior so that you can take steps to head off these behaviors before they become a problem? What are you going to do if you feel yourself getting frustrated or losing your temper? Make yourself a note that says, "Take a break," and one that says, "Go to the balcony," and put them where you can see them during the meeting.

If you are weak on some aspect of the deal, you can (a) make yourself smarter on whatever it is, or (b) bring along a subject matter expert. Preparation gives you confidence, and confidence gives you power.

If you can work out these details and others like them in advance, you will remove a lot of the pressure that you normally feel when walking into what you know will be a tough negotiation.

> ➤ PROFESSIONAL NEGOTIATING TIP
>
> Preparation gives you confidence, and confidence gives you power.

How to Hang on to Power When the Action Gets Heavy

Even if you do everything we recommend and walk into that conference room with your head held high and plenty of confidence, there is no guarantee that you will hang on to your power once things get rolling.

We have already outlined some of the many tactics and strategies that buyers will use to deliberately knock you off your game plan.

Quite often, their goal is to confuse, obfuscate, frustrate, bully, annoy, or otherwise rattle you. They know that an emotional negotiator is an ineffective one. If you are going to keep your cool under duress, you need a plan.

In Chapter 3, we gave you some ideas on how to deal with bullies. In Chapter 5, we talked about tactics and countertactics. This is where all of that will pay off for you. If you can keep track of what is going on around the table (don't forget to watch those nonverbals from chapter 6), you will not only be able to deal with the gamesmanship from the other side, but you will be able to monitor your position and intervene early on if you sense a problem developing.

For instance, let's say that the buyer is using tactics aimed at deliberately making you angry. And the tactics are working! By "going to the balcony" (Chapter 3), you will see that you are becoming emotional and you need to suggest taking a break.

By seizing control and breaking the negative momentum, you can get out of the room and away from the confrontational situation before you fall into the buyer's trap and make a bad decision based on emotion.

The added benefit of calling for a break at this point is that it puts you in control of the agenda. You ask for a time-out. You decide how long to stay out of the room. You walk back in and say something like, "Okay. Now, where were we?" Who's got the power now? You do!

There are other methods that you can use to take or keep power in negotiations, and we will discuss them in more detail in just a moment. The learning point here is that if you feel you are losing power, you probably are. Unless you do something differently, you will keep losing it and can get hurt in the negotiation.

Now let's talk about power plays that you are likely to encounter and what to do about them.

Title Power

Have you ever walked into a meeting and been surprised to find a senior manager or company official on the other side of the table? It can be quite unnerving to prepare for a meeting with a buyer and find yourself negotiating with a "C-level" executive. Companies will sometimes do this as a way to intimidate or pressure salespeople.

This isn't likely to happen to you, because you are always going to call first and find out who is going to be present at the meeting. Doing this gives you the chance to balance titles and subject matter expertise on your side of the table. When you set up the meeting, always ask, "Will anyone else be joining us?" Of course, it isn't always practical or even desirable to lug along the president of your company (or even your immediate supervisor) on a sales call, so what are you going to do?

If you decide to make a solo sales call and you know that you will be facing senior managers, or if you get surprised and find them at the table, you always want to keep two things in mind. First, thank your lucky stars that you took the time to properly prepare and plan for this meeting. Your notes and planning sheets will allow you to stick with your game plan. You will come across as a professional and serious business partner and not as an easily rattled rookie salesperson. Second, if the president or any other high-ranking executive of a client company takes the time to show up at your meeting with a buyer, it means that whatever you are selling is important to her. She thinks you have something that can help the company with a need, or she wouldn't be there. The fact this discussion is important enough for her to sit in means that this is potentially a big deal for her, and that knowledge gives you . . . that's right . . . power!

Expertise Power

You'll see this power play when the client or buyer brings in some kind of a subject matter expert (SME). If he brings a logistics whiz with him, chances are that he is going to want to really get into nitty-gritty detail on how things get done. If logistics is one of your strong suits, great. If it's not, you had better bring someone with you who is a logistics whiz so that she can answer questions from the client's SME. Otherwise, the client is going to make you feel inadequate, and you will have a hard time controlling the flow of your meeting.

Fortunately the antidote to this is simple. Again, you ask, up front, for a list of the names and titles of the people who will be in attendance. Review the list, and bring along anyone that you need from your company to balance out the expertise on both sides. Quite often, the SMEs will have their own side conversations going, and the meeting will be productive because a multitude of issues can be discussed and resolved at one time.

One final thought on expertise power: if you ever walk into a conference room and find out that the other side has brought an attorney (unannounced), that is a *huge* red flag! Lawyers introduce a whole new level of complexity and risk into a negotiation, and you are not trained or qualified to discuss legal matters with them. You need to tell your counterpart immediately that you are not authorized by your company to make legal commitments and that if there are legal matters to discuss, you will need to reschedule the meeting when you can return with your own counsel. Either you go or they go! Remember, it's okay to be positional (C1) in cases where not being positional can cause you and your company harm. You can even suggest that the lawyer can stay, as long as he doesn't "go legal" on you.

"Name-Dropping" Power

You are most likely to see this power play in an internal negotiation. Your coworker might turn to you and say, "You know, Phil [big guy, corner office] was really hoping that you could get this forecast done by Monday." In other words, your peer doesn't have the juice to get you to do it on his own so he is using somebody else's clout to get you to do it.

Now, if Phil in the corner office really wants it done, you had probably better bite the bullet and work this weekend. However, if your colleague is just dropping Phil's name, maybe you decide to play golf. You really need to know what's going on in your company to make the call on this one.

Recognize this gambit for what it is and react accordingly.

Quite often, salespeople find their toughest negotiations are internal. Getting the "doers" to do what they are supposed to be doing isn't as easy as it ought to be. Here are some tips to help you with your internal negotiations.

Conditional Power

Someone who usually doesn't have much power is able to exert this type of power over you because of the specific circumstances in which you find yourself. Think of the clerk in the post office who is working at half speed. It doesn't matter who you are or what you do for a living, if you are in that line, you aren't going anywhere until that clerk says, "Next."

Let us illustrate with another example:

Several years ago, one of our partners and his wife traveled to Westchester County, New York. Our partner's father-in-law had passed away, and they needed to go up to his home and settle some of his affairs.

An old family friend offered to take the couple to lunch at a very exclusive golf club at which the father-in-law had been a member for many years. As they settled into their chairs in the dining room and admired the immaculately maintained course outside, the friend nudged our partner and pointed to a distinguished-looking waitress on the other side of the room.

"That's Helen," he said. "She's been here for over twenty years. On Tuesdays and Thursdays she's here in the dining room. On Mondays, Wednesdays, and Fridays she works the switchboard."

Our partner nodded politely and picked up his menu. The friend wasn't finished yet. He continued, "About a month ago, while Helen was working the switchboard, she took an unusual call. The caller identified himself as working at the White House. He said that [then] President Clinton would be visiting his new home in Chappaqua the following week and that he would like to come by the club and play the course."

Helen, he said, did not miss a beat. "And which of our members will he be playing with?" she politely inquired.

There was a long pause, and then the caller cleared his throat and said, "Perhaps you misunderstood what I said. President Clinton would like to play your course."

"No," said Helen, "you were perfectly clear. As are our rules, which state that any guest must be accompanied by a member in good standing."

There was another long pause, and the caller then hung up. President Clinton did not play the course, and Helen became an instant star among the (almost exclusively Republican) club members.

When the switchboard operator of a private club can tell the leader of the free world to go hack around a public course—that's conditional power!

Being aware of conditional power is the first step. The next step is making sure you use that very power in your favor. Make sure the person with the conditional power knows that you realize he is in control of this situation. Ask, "How would you recommend we solve this issue?" This person may often be ignored, and some TLC and diplomacy will help you get him on your side. Trying to go around him or pushing him will just lead to his unleashing more of his precious conditional power.

As an example, a startlingly high percentage of executives end up marrying their administrative assistants. The sales rep who tries to bully or trick the gatekeeper will probably end up out on his ear. It is much better to treat everyone within a client's organization with respect and deference.

The Power of the Written Word

Anything written has more power than anything spoken! Remember the processing fee sign at the car dealership? Plenty of people see the sign and begrudgingly pay the $299. Why? Because the sign makes it official. We don't even think about this subtle power in a negotiation. How many times during a negotiation has one side completely stopped the other side by reaching into a briefcase and presenting "the document" that clearly says this issue has to be resolved this way?

Another form of written power comes in the font size! A 12- or 14-point font looks like a draft, and people will argue about that written point for days. Change the font to 8 or 9 point, and it suddenly has more clout. Why? It looks more legal and official.

As we pointed out earlier, salespeople can use written power effectively by taking notes during a negotiation, preparing the summary, and sending all the attendees the notes. It is easier to put your spin on the meeting than try to change someone else's, especially a customer's.

There are many more types of power plays, but you should get the idea by now. Your customers may well try to use power games to knock you off your game plan. Remember these things about power:

+ Power is largely perceptual. If you think that you've got it, you probably do. If you think that you don't have it, you don't.

+ Power is fluid. Just because you have it now doesn't mean you will have it later. You need to constantly monitor the power situation in a negotiation. If you have it, then go full speed ahead. If you are losing it, then you need to do something to break the momentum and get it back.

+ Planning gives you power. The better prepared you are for the negotiation, the more confidence and power you will have going in.

+ Alternatives give you power.

+ Having a walkaway figure gives you power because you know that you aren't going to get carried away and do something stupid.

+ You must recognize and deal with the tactics that the other side uses to try to take your power away.

+ You are a professional, and you have a right to be there.

CHAPTER 12

WHY WON'T WE
ASK WHY?

Our customers often take positions with us, for example:

+ I won't pay more than X for your product.
+ I have to have the shipment by next Tuesday.
+ We want to return all of the unsold inventory.
+ We want a guaranteed low price.
+ I want price protection for at least twelve months.

It should be obvious why positions can be problematic to us as sellers. So how do you get away from positions and into a collaborative mode? It starts with a basic understanding that, for the most part, statements create positions, and positions hamper the ability of any negotiator to be collaborative. So the fewer statements you or the other side makes, the greater the opportunity for a collaborative negotiation.

Usually the role of moving toward a collaborative solution will fall on the shoulders of the seller. Therefore, sellers must know how to uncover what is motivating the other person to take her position. They must then creatively work toward a solution.

We had a situation a few years ago involving one of our senior partners that illustrates this concept:

Equipment supplied to a major utility (nuclear power plant) experienced out-of-warranty product problems that cost the utility hundreds of millions of dollars in equipment repair and replacement power costs. The utility's position was that the equipment was sold with a forty-year expected service life. Regardless of warranty period expiration, the utility demanded that the manufacturer pay for all repairs and replacement power. Replacement power costs alone were more than $1 million per day. Equipment repairs and replacement were estimated at $150 million.

The manufacturer refused to pay any costs, based upon warranty expiration and the customer's poor maintenance and operating procedures. Meeting after meeting went nowhere except to make tempers more frayed and volatile.

Eventually the customer threatened to sue the manufacturer. As more and more tension entered the situation, the manufacturer threatened to pull operational support from the site unless the customer agreed to pay for services. The manufacturer sent in the sales organization to deliver that message to the customer.

The utility decided that the sales organization was not acting as a customer advocate and demanded that the manufacturer remove the local management and sales team from all its sites. The manufacturer pulled the entire sales team and replaced the sales manager with a new person who had no experience in the nuclear field.

Being new, the replacement sales manager had an informal meeting with the utility executives to find out how things had gotten so screwed up.

He asked a simple question: "Why is all of this happening?"

During the discussions, he found out that the customer had experienced problems with the manufacturer's equipment at other nuclear stations. Federal and state regulators had chastised the utility for poor management practices. People were let go or demoted, and careers were destroyed over these issues. Current managers were not going to let that happen to them.

The new sales manager then visited with his nuclear executives to learn how and why things had gotten to that point. He discovered that the manufacturer had more than thirty nuclear power plants with the same equipment. If they gave in to this customer, billions of dollars in claims were at stake across the world. It could bankrupt the company.

The manager then met with the president of the utility to get his perspective of the situation. He discovered that the president was an ex-manager from this same manufacturer, and he personally felt let down by the entire state of affairs. He further said that he expected the sales organization to remain neutral and try to help resolve issues rather than act as another member of the manufacturer's negotiating team espousing the same line as the manufacturing business unit.

The new sales manager then talked with his president and received permission to act in the neutral position (as requested by the customer). He replaced all the people on his staff who were "tainted" by the situation.

In response, the president of the utility said that he would stop litigation plans and continue talks with the manufacturer. He also agreed to replace all utility individuals who were considered biased.

Once the motivating factors (interests) had been discovered, work began on a framework agreement between the customer's executive vice president of nuclear power and the sales manager. It involved the first ever Partnership in Performance program in the USA. The manufacturer provided equipment and services at a discount to get the units back up to operational excellence, and the customer agreed to give the manufacturer all service and equipment work on a no-bid basis for the life of the plant. If the customer followed the manufacturer's procedures and recommendations, any restorative work was to be done at a 70 percent discount off list price. If the customer refused to comply with the manufacturer's recommendations and the equipment failed due to that decision, the customer would pay for services and equipment at full list price. The manufacturer placed people on-site as part of the customer's team, and customer personnel were assigned to the manufacturer's business unit as part of their team.

During the dispute, business with the utility had dropped from more than $100 million per year to less than $10 million. As a result of the new arrangement, business was back at $100 million within two years. By the end of year five, the manufacturer was enjoying a 100 percent market share of all business, nuclear and nonnuclear, at all the customer sites. Bookings grew to $800 million.

This multimillion-dollar situation could have ruined two large businesses. It began to move away from positions and toward a collaborative solution only when someone asked two *why* questions! Amazing, isn't it? It seems so simple. Yet we know from experience just how hard it is for many salespeople to ask that first *why* question.

Why do salespeople have trouble asking a *why* question? We have discovered these reasons:

+ Salespeople feel that they are supposed to already know why.
+ Salespeople feel that asking why could be perceived as too direct.
+ Salespeople don't want to appear to be dumb.
+ Salespeople may be afraid of the answer.
+ Salespeople want to address the stated position with comments,

such as, "It's impossible to get it there by Thursday," or "You are already getting our best price."

Even though it may be difficult, we encourage salespeople to explore what is motivating a customer's statement or position. Sometimes your client will refuse to give you a straight answer to a *why* question. She might say, "Because that's how it's got to be," or something equally unhelpful. What if you can't ask why? What can you do?

Here's a list of questions/statements that might help you separate the motivating factors from the positions:

+ We appreciate what you've done/are trying to do.
+ We would like to settle this on the basis of principle, not on the basis of selfish interest or power.
+ Trust is a separate issue.
+ May I ask you a few questions to determine if my facts are correct?
+ What's the principle behind your thoughts?
+ Let me see if I understand what you're saying . . .
+ Let me get back to you on that by . . .
+ Let me explain why I have trouble following some of your reasoning.
+ Is a trial basis/period possible?
+ If we disagree, the inferences are . . .
+ What are you trying to accomplish by . . . ?
+ Could you reword your proposal?
+ Could you tell me what we both can gain by your proposal?
+ Let me see if I understand your concern. . . .
+ Would you consider . . . ?
+ Could you tell me what problems you see with my proposal?
+ How can we decide what is reasonable? What is fair?
+ Can we break the issue down into more manageable parts?

✦ I understand that's your position, but could you explain what you are concerned about?

And consider using the negative side to explore for the motivating factor. If a person won't tell you why, maybe he will "spill the beans" if you make a statement and then ask, "Why won't this work?" Many people love to tell you why something won't work. If you listen carefully, you might just hear what's behind their position.

One of the authors was involved recently with the launch of a new-to-the-world consumer goods product. When his client presented it to the buyer for a retail grocery chain, the buyer turned him down.

When asked why, the buyer stated that he liked the product very much but that it was seasonal and they were too late into the season to add a new item. The buyer's interest was in not getting stuck with unsold inventory at the end of the season. When our client offered to take back any unsold product and waive restocking charges, the buyer placed an immediate order. Not only that, but he arranged to have freestanding in-store displays set up.

Another technique is the layered approach to questioning. Don't ask just one question and expect to get all the motivation behind that position. Most of the time, you will need to follow one question with a more specific question, followed by another question, and so on.

The next time you hear a customer state, "Well, the payment terms will be ninety days," don't argue about the unfairness of that position or the ten reasons why the customer shouldn't do that. Ask why and wait for the answer.

Using Frames to Uncover Motivation

And consider framing when you're trying to unlock the motivating factor behind a position. Frames are perspectives through which we view a negotiation. Each side will have its own view of the issues, and not surprisingly, they will often view the same issues in very different ways. These frames are created by values, experiences, and beliefs, so it is perfectly logical for different parties to bring diverse frames of reference to the negotiating table.

Frames are sometimes defined as "collections of perceptions and thoughts that people use to define a situation, organize information, and determine what is important and what is not." We create frames to name a situation in which we find ourselves, to identify and interpret specific aspects that seem key to us in understanding the situation, and to communicate that interpretation to others.

Another way to say this is: all of us look at the world (or any situation we are negotiating) through our own set of filters. Some of these filters or frames might be

+ *Power*. Many people will look at every element of the negotiation in terms of whether it enhances or diminishes their power.
+ *Risk*. Everyone has a different tolerance for risk, and people will look at deals on the basis of risk/reward.
+ *Background*. Personal experience, good or bad, will affect how individuals approach their negotiations.
+ *Ethics*. It is helpful but not absolutely necessary if both sides share similar values.
+ *Trust*. Some of us are very trusting. Some of us aren't.

Applying the Concept of Frames and Filters

First, recognize that each party is entering the discussion with his or her own set of frames. If the frames are similar, then the likelihood of reaching an agreement is greatly enhanced. If the frames are opposite or significantly different, the likelihood of reaching an agreement is probably inversely proportional to the degree of the differences.

Second, since framing is a part of all negotiations, you may need to reframe some issues in order to move closer to an agreement. Reframing means recognizing that the frame you are using may be inappropriate or unproductive for your current situation. Sometimes it is as simple as having each party state what he is looking for in the negotiations. You can then identify your areas of agreement and those that will need more discussion. It can also be very difficult: for instance, if one or both parties decide not to disclose why they have taken a certain position.

Reframing uses a number of the skills we have discussed previously:

+ asking questions
+ listening
+ selecting a topic and brainstorming a solution
+ tabling a difficult issue so you can move on
+ taking a break to refocus
+ clarifying and expanding on a topic
+ discovering the motivation

Third, when issues appear too difficult to resolve, step back and look at the framing from your point of view and that of the person sitting across from you. Ask yourself this question: "Are we really talking about the same issue?"

Sometimes, the parties are so intent on making their points that they talk past each other and don't really communicate. When this happens, the result is generally frustration and some kind of an impasse. To avoid this, you've got to focus on the intent behind the words. Look for common ground. If you can't find it using the frames that you brought into the meeting, start reframing. In there, somewhere, may be a solution.

CHAPTER 13

YOUR NEGOTIATING TEAM: GODSEND OR DISASTER? IT'S UP TO YOU

BRINGING A TEAM IS A GOOD IDEA WHEN YOU ARE ENTER-
ing complicated or critically important negotiations. Properly utilized, a
team can be more creative, more effective, and more efficient than any
one individual. Notice that we said "properly utilized." Like any of the
other negotiation skill sets, team negotiating requires logic and planning
in order to pay off. Simply showing up with a bunch of people can be a
huge waste of time and resources. In this chapter, we will discuss the key
elements of team negotiating.

Most salespeople can come up with plenty of examples of a team
strategy backfiring on them. Years ago, one of the authors was making
an important customer call to discuss a large order for plastic products.
He decided to bring along a materials engineer in case the discussion
became technical. As expected, the client balked at the premium prices
charged by the author's company. In an effort to be helpful, the engineer
chimed in to say, "Our products contain hardly any regrind [reprocessed

material]." Since 100 percent virgin resin was one of the company's key selling points, "hardly any" was not only unhelpful, but it sidetracked the meeting in an extremely negative direction.

If you are going to have a team, you need to manage it and direct it to avoid a disaster like this.

How Do I Know If I Need a Team?

We have alluded to this question in earlier chapters. Now let's face it head-on. In order to know whether you should bring anyone with you, you need the answers to two questions:

1. Who's going to be there on the buyer's side of the table?
2. What do they want to talk about?

How do you find out this stuff in advance? You call and ask. For example, if you find out that the client is going to have an IT person there and IT isn't your strong suit, then you had better bring someone along who can answer the questions, or it's not going to be a very productive meeting. If the client is going to have an attorney there, then you definitely shouldn't show up without your own lawyer in tow.

How Many People Do I Want on My Team?

There are no hard-and-fast rules on this, but it is usually a mistake to try to overwhelm the other side with a big contingent from your company. If the customer has two representatives at the table and you show up with twelve, you are sending a message that your company isn't very efficient and your managers don't have much authority to act on their own.

We think that except in rare cases, it is a mistake to outnumber the other side by more than one. If they've got two people there, having three is probably okay for you. Any more than that smacks of overkill and inefficiency.

Team Strategy

Successful teams are not put together haphazardly or as a show of force. Everyone on your team should be there for a reason, and each person should know exactly what that reason is long before you leave your office. You want to balance the customer's subject matter experts with your own. If decisions are likely to be made that you don't have the authority to make, then you need to bring along someone who does.

All team members should know what issues will be discussed, and they should know how and where they will be expected to contribute to the discussion. They should also know the roles of the other team members and what each of them should and shouldn't talk about. The last thing you need is some technical type talking about pricing or marketing matters (see the example at the beginning of this chapter).

It is a good idea to appoint someone on your team as the designated note taker. Doing this frees up the other team members to concentrate on what is going on in the negotiation. The note taker can also be one of the subject matter experts.

Team Leader

Every team needs a clearly defined leader, and contrary to common practice, the leader isn't necessarily the most senior team member. The leader ought to be the person with the deepest knowledge of the client. Often that will be the local salesperson or regional sales manager.

Resist the temptation to line up your team like chessmen on a board. Doing this is counterproductive and confrontational.

A much better approach is to intersperse your team with theirs. This arrangement allows for a more collaborative and less "us vs. them" setup, but, more important, it lets you maintain eye contact with the other members of your team.

If the table is round, the same logic applies. Try to sit in such a way as to keep your team in sight at all times. If possible, try to seat subject matter experts together so that they can have separate sidebar conversations without distracting the entire group.

Power Seating

If you are meeting in your customer's conference room, particularly if the room is just off an executive's private office, you can be pretty sure that A is where the executive likes to sit. Don't sit there.

You are much better off going to B or D. If you sit in A, you have trespassed on your customer's territory, and it will probably make him uncomfortable or angry. If you sit in C, you have created an adversarial arrangement with the two of you facing each other across the table. B and D are better because you are in a more collaborative and consultative position.

Where you sit does matter, and it shouldn't be random. Plan, in advance, where each member should sit vis-à-vis the counterpart on the other side.

Team Signals

In team negotiations, working out a few simple, nonverbal signals in advance is wise. Kicking someone under the table might be an effective way to get him to shut up, but it isn't very professional. And when he screams or winces, you have told the other side that they are getting information you don't want them to have.

Although it would be nice, you can't have twenty-five different signals for your team. Having more than three tends to be confusing. Your team members will get them mixed up, and you will look like a third-base coach running through a complicated series of signals for the batter.

For most meetings, three basic signals are enough. We recommend these:

1. Stop talking now!
2. I want to take a break as soon as this point is complete, so don't start a new topic.
3. Turn over the conversation to me.

These are universal enough to cover most occasions when you want to communicate with your team without speaking. To get these points across, we use a signal pen. The signal pen is really nothing more than an extra writing instrument. The only thing that makes it special is that you don't actually write with it. You place it in plain sight near your notes and writing pad, but you use another pen to take notes.

No one on the other side will pay any attention to an extra pen on the table, but your team will be trained to keep an eye on it. For example, if you decide that you want to take a break, you would pick up the signal pen, fiddle with it for a moment so that all of your team members were aware of it, and then put it in your pocket. Now they know that you are anxious to take a break, and they know not to start a new conversational thread. As soon as someone on either side pauses, you are going to ask for a time-out and get out of there.

The same idea works for "stop talking now!" If someone on your team is heading for dangerous territory, you can pick up the signal pen and stand it on its end. At the same time, you can give her a good hard stare so she knows to look for a signal. If she is properly trained, she will get the message and shut up. This is a lot more subtle and elegant than giving her a shot under the table, and it works just as well.

The team leader should also have a signal for "give the ball back to me." Sometimes team members can get carried away, and it is useful to be able to reassert control without making them look bad. The signal could be as simple as pointing the signal pen back at yourself.

You can use more signals if you want, but we strongly recommend that you limit the number to avoid chaos. It is extremely useful sometimes to be able to communicate with your team without tipping off the other side. Needless to say, this kind of thing needs to be an integral part of the planning process and not something that you ad-lib.

Summary

A team can be a powerful negotiation tool or a big waste of everyone's time. It is the job of the team leader to make sure that all of the members know why they are on the team and what is expected of them during the negotiations.

Don't forget about taking breaks. If your team strategy isn't working or some new and unanticipated development crops up, call for a break and huddle with your team to make sure everyone is still on the same page. If the negotiations are going to be protracted, you might even ask the other side to designate a room for you to use. This is better than standing around in the hall discussing your next move.

A little time spent up front on planning and preparation will pay big dividends when the action starts to heat up. The difference between the pros and the wannabes is in the details.

CHAPTER 14

CREATIVITY: THE BEST NEGOTIATOR'S SECRET OF SUCCESS

CREATIVITY ISN'T USUALLY MENTIONED IN THE SAME breath as negotiations. This is unfortunate because it is a critical skill set in the master negotiator's arsenal. Let's face it. Sometimes you get stuck. Despite all of your planning, your strategizing, your what-if work, things just grind to a halt. Sometimes the culprit is a big issue like price, terms, or delivery date. Sometimes it's something relatively minor like package layout or pack size. Either way, in a complex negotiation, there are literally hundreds of details, big and small, that can gum up your deal.

When that happens, you can call on several skill sets that we have already discussed to get things moving again. You can take a break. You can change someone or something about the deal. Or you can harness the brainpower sitting around the table and come up with a solution that isn't immediately obvious but satisfies the interests of both sides.

Let us give you a couple of quick examples of how this might work:

One of our associates has a good friend who is a commercial property manager. He is responsible for the overall operation of several office buildings in Richmond, Virginia. He came to us with a problem he was having in one of the older buildings that he managed.

His tenants were angry because they felt that the old elevator in the building was costing them time and money. The elevator had been installed years ago, and though properly maintained, it was quite a bit slower than newer models. The tenants felt that their employees and clients were wasting precious time each day waiting for this old elevator to take them up and down to their floors. They had circulated a petition among themselves threatening not to renew their leases unless the building's owners found a way to speed up the elevator or replaced it.

When our friend took the petition to the owner, he was told that the elevator was still in good shape and he had no intention of replacing it; it was moving as fast as it was designed to go and couldn't be sped up, and it was his (our friend's) job to figure out how to make the tenants happy.

We brainstormed the problem with our friend, we talked to knowledgeable people in the industry, and we came up with a solution that made everyone happy and cost less than $200.

Want to guess what he did?

He put a large mirror in the elevator lobby. Now, in the morning, people don't stand around and look at their watches, muttering evil things about the landlord. No, they check out their makeup/necktie/front teeth/and so forth in the new mirror, and before they know it, the elevator is there to whisk them up to their floor.

Problem solved by creative thinking. The answer wasn't obvious, but it was there. It usually is out there somewhere.

We used this story in a class in Rome several years ago, and when we got through, a hand went up in the back of the room. A sales rep from Zurich said that he had a similar example. Here's his story:

The International Terminal at the Zurich Airport was constantly generating passenger complaints regarding the time it took for luggage to appear on the carousel in customs. Passengers would deplane, many of them tired and grouchy from overnight flights, and proceed fairly quickly through immigration. Once they got to the customs area, however, the wait for bags seemed endless.

Investigation by the airport's managers revealed that little could be done to speed up the baggage handlers, the conveyor belts, or the trams bringing the bags from the planes to the terminal. All were working about as fast as they could reasonably be expected to work.

After a lot of head-scratching and brainstorming, the managers came up with a great solution that didn't cost anything.

What did they do?

They rerouted arriving international passengers through the terminal. The new layout takes an extra five to ten minutes to walk. Now, when passengers pass through immigration and head for customs, they are likely to find their bags already circulating on the carousel.

Travelers leave the terminal building expressing nothing but admiration for the efficiency of the Swiss aviation system.

Isn't creativity great?

We like these examples because, in both cases, the solutions are outside the box and probably wouldn't come up during typical discussions of the problems. In order to arrive at creative solutions like these, you need to do several things differently:

+ Include as many people as practical in the process. Sometimes people who aren't subject matter experts are particularly helpful because they aren't hamstrung by preconceived notions.
+ Begin by describing the problem to the team, and then solicit ideas. Accept their ideas in a noncritical way. Just laundry-list

them on a flip chart or a whiteboard, and make sure that everyone involved understands them.

+ Involve your customer in this process if possible. It is a great way to establish a collaborative atmosphere for the rest of the negotiation. Also, any solutions that the client had a hand in developing will be much easier to implement down the road.

+ Make sure that everyone knows there are no stupid ideas—the wilder they are, the better.

+ Be very inclusive, not exclusive, with ideas from the group. Encourage the quiet people to speak up. Sometimes they have great ideas but are too shy to say anything without prompting.

+ Go back through each idea on the list, and ask, "Could this work?"

+ Take parts of one idea, combine them with something from somewhere else, and come up with a completely unique solution. Try refining the ideas and looking for ways to make them work.

Sometimes the best ideas are the most outlandish. Let's look at another example:

The Sydney Harbor Bridge ranks as one of the engineering marvels of the world. It is a towering structure, rising 440 feet above the busy Sydney Harbor. At almost three-fourths of a mile in length, it is the world's largest steel-arch bridge, and it provides a spectacular backdrop to the Opera House in countless photographs and videos of Sydney's famous harbor.

Since it opened in 1932, the bridge has been extremely busy as well as photogenic. Today, it handles more than 150,000 vehicles per day. The combination of this heavy traffic and the corrosive effects of the environment takes a toll on the bridge. Maintenance is never ending and expensive. Repainting it takes 10 years and 21,000 gallons of paint. The

6 million rivets that hold it together need regular replacement. Altogether, it costs well over $5 million per year to keep the structure in good condition.

This expense is a considerable burden on the city's budget. In 1989, local entrepreneur Paul Cave approached the city council with an idea for a revenue-sharing business venture to help defray the maintenance expenses. His idea was so outlandish that he was laughed out of the meeting. Not one to give up easily, Cave spent the next nine years lobbying various state and local officials to get a fair hearing for his idea. Because his venture was so unconventional, the conservative government types in charge of the permits and licenses couldn't visualize how it would work.

Finally he more or less wore down all of the skeptics who had been in his way, and on October 1, 1998, he kicked off the new venture.

What was his idea?

Cave proposed to charge tourists a lot of money to strap themselves to the superstructure and walk over the top of the arch.

It's a crazy idea. Who in his right mind would want to climb more than forty-four stories into the air, chained to a bridge, pelted by the elements, and pay big money to do it?

According to people who have actually made the climb, the panoramic view of the harbor is more than worth the effort. To most of us, just the thought of it seems ridiculous. So how did it work out?

If you look closely at the bridge today, you might be able to see what looks like a steady stream of ants crawling along the top. All day long you can see these specks moving from one end of the arch to the other.

For more than $100 per person, Cave's company, BridgeClimb, outfits hardy adventurers with a special jumpsuit, a safety harness, a radio, a hat, a hanky, a raincoat (in wet weather), and a head light (for evening climbs). Then in groups of twelve, guides lead these brave souls on a three-and-a-half-hour walk across the top of the bridge's super-structure.

As of June 2005, BridgeClimb had sold more than 1.5 million trips. If you want to take one of these tours, you need to make your reservation weeks in advance. Groups leave at ten-minute intervals from dusk until late into the evening. The tours run 363 days per year.

The runaway success of this wild idea has brought fame and fortune to Cave (and a lot of incremental revenue to Sydney). And it's all because he looked at things a little differently from everyone else and then had the guts to keep pushing his idea in the faces of a lot of conventional thinkers. Great salespeople don't give up just because other people can't or won't see the benefits of their ideas.

The best ideas aren't always immediately obvious, and they don't necessarily come from the usual sources. When things grind to a halt, the team leader must take advantage of all the experience and creativity that he can in order to come up with a new solution to get things moving again.

CHAPTER 15

CONCLUDING THE
DEAL—FINALLY

So now it's all smiles around the table. Hands have been shaken; dotted lines have been signed; backs have been slapped. Nothing left to do now but gather up your stuff and head out for a celebratory drink, right?

Wrong.

Lots of good deals get messed up at exactly this point. Sometimes sellers (and buyers) are in such a hurry to get out of the room that they leave loose ends hanging around. Unless you take a few more minutes to wrap things up completely, you are opening the door for potential problems down the road. The bigger and more complicated the deal, the more important this next step is.

Even though a contract is a contract and a purchase order is a purchase order, there is almost always a gray area around a deal, particularly a big deal. You will save yourself a lot of time and trouble if you just take a few more minutes and do these things:

Summarize the Agreement

On a separate sheet of paper, write down what each party has agreed to do in order to make your deal happen. This is critical because people tend to remember what they want to remember. Quite often, the actual implementation steps (who is going to set up your product numbers in the system and by when, for example) are not spelled out in the contract. Or if the other side really hated to give up on a particular point, their memory might get a little fuzzy on the specifics in the time between verbal agreement and formal contract.

Since you have been taking the notes (see Chapter 11), it should be easy for you to put together a recap of what each party has agreed to. In some cases it is appropriate to ask both parties to sign or initial this document. At other times it is easier to mail or e-mail the recap to all of the parties involved in the deal.

This step will protect you from

+ selective memory problems on either side.
+ the buyer reneging on an oral commitment made during the negotiation.
+ shifting priorities that pull people away from your project.
+ personnel changes that impact your deal. If the buyer is replaced, a written record of the negotiation will prevent you from having to start all over again.

The document itself should be the essence of simplicity. In clear and straightforward language, it should spell out the specifics of what each party has agreed to. Here are examples of things that the agreement might contain:

+ pricing and price protection (if any)
+ quantities and quantity pricing levels

- delivery dates and lead times
- item numbers, colors, carton packs, and minimum orders
- annual purchase levels (if applicable)
- payment terms and conditions
- "ship to" locations and freight policies
- penalties for noncompliance
- program review dates (monthly, quarterly, annually)
- contact information for key personnel at both buyer's and seller's companies
- any late fees or penalties
- upcharges for custom colors, packs, or other special requests

Your goal for this document is to put together a description of the deal that is detailed enough for a new employee to read it and understand who has agreed to what. Doing this may seem like additional work, but think about it: things change, people change. That buyer may do twenty more deals after you walk out of his conference room. Do you really want to trust your bonus to his memory?

Another benefit of doing this yourself is that you can make darn sure that the things you want included in the deal are in there. A little more effort at this point can save you a ton of grief later. It is also a nice, professional touch that will help set you apart from your competition.

Develop an Action Plan

Usually a negotiated agreement leads to "to do" lists for both sides. It is a bad idea to assume that each side is clear on the next steps. You need to write them down. The best time to do this is while everything is still fresh in everyone's mind. You will be amazed at how quickly people can get wrapped up in something else and forget about your deal and what they ought to be doing to move it along. If time doesn't permit you to put the plan together on the spot, then set a date very soon to reconvene and get it done. The sooner the better.

An action plan doesn't have to be elaborate. It is a simple document that summarizes who has agreed to do what and by when. Both parties may add to it as specific assignments are delegated within their organizations. The important point is to have a timeline with specific events and people identified for the project.

Highlighting milestones for management review can keep a project on track and can uncover potential problems before they become nasty surprises.

A portion of a typical action plan might look like this:

Project: Mega Office/Amigo Product Rollout

EVENT	DESCRIPTION	RESPONSIBLE	COMPLETION
1	Mega issues POs w/ shipping information & quantities per location to Amigo.	Henderson	8/15/2006
2	Mega creates SKUs and warehouse locations for Amigo items.	Henderson	8/30/2006
3	Amigo sets up Mega in accounting system.	Smith	8/30/2006
4	Mega e-mails usage forecast for Amigo.	Henderson	9/1/2006
5	Mega notifies store managers to begin clearing out old PDAs.	Henderson	9/15/2006
6	Amigo begins shipping product & in-store merchandising materials to Mega.	Jones	9/30/2006
7	All product received at Mega locations.	Jones	10/15/2006
8	90-day review of product movement.	Smith/ Henderson	1/15/2007

Project: Mega Office/Amigo Product Rollout

Make sure that everyone involved in making your deal happen gets copied on the plan. That way, problems can be identified early on, and actions can be taken to get things back on track. People are much more likely to perform if they know that they are being measured and held accountable on a timeline. The more specific you can be about who is going to do what needs to be done, the more likely your program will run smoothly. That makes you look good inside and outside your company. It also makes your customer look good, and that's the best way there is to get more business!

Make Sure the Other Party Feels Good About the Deal

Be sure to compliment the client on what a good job he did for his company. He ought to feel as good about the outcome as you do. You can use objective criteria to show the client how favorably the deal stacks up against others. Examples of the criteria might be industry averages (cost per square foot, cost as a percentage of sales, ROI, etc.) and actual vs. estimated or budgeted cost.

You can say something like, "We are really pleased that we could work this deal out, and we're looking forward to working with you to make it happen. You should be proud of the job that you did for your company. Usually a project like this comes in at about $140 per square foot. You've been able to get it done for $119 per square foot. Congratulations!"

Try to give the client something that he can take back to his peers to show how and why this is a good deal.

Conduct a Win-Loss Review

It's almost time to start celebrating—but not quite. Many companies do postmortems on lost business. The best companies also do a review on deals that they win. While all of the details are fresh in everyone's mind, you need to review the results and ask a few questions:

+ Why did we win (or lose) this one? Was it price, features, delivery dates?
+ Did we leave money on the table?
+ Did our competitors do anything new or unexpected on this one?
+ What should we do differently next time?

And last but not least: We usually try to make our negotiations collaborative. How do we know if this particular deal was done collaboratively? In *Getting to Yes*, William Ury and Roger Fisher suggest three questions:

1. Was the deal concluded in a time-efficient manner?
2. Was the end result satisfactory to both parties?
3. Is the relationship with the client at least as strong (if not stronger) now than it was before we began the negotiation?

If the answer was yes to all three, congratulations! You have just had a truly collaborative experience.

Now, it's time to go out and celebrate!

CHAPTER 16

WHAT DO YOU MEAN, I'M IN A REVERSE AUCTION?

BARRY, THE OWNER OF BEST PRINTERS, INC., A SUCCESSFUL local printing firm, wanted to break into the seemingly lucrative world of large commercial printing. He was excited about being invited to his first online auction. Not ever having been in an online auction, Barry went to the suggested Web site hosted by the company running the auction (for the unknown customer) and read about the rules and procedures. The auction started, and after the first round, Barry felt pretty good as six of the ten potential printers had dropped out after the initial reduction of only 15 percent (Best Printers, Inc., had always enjoyed much higher margins, and 15 percent less wasn't that bad).

Following the second round, again Barry was elated when there were only three bidders and the reduction was 27 percent off Barry's list price. The end of the third round left only Barry and one competitor. Things were getting serious. The competitive bid that showed up next nearly knocked Barry off his chair: it was 43 percent off his list price and more than 8 percent lower than any price he'd ever offered! Barry thought long and hard before he made his last bid of 46 percent off his list price. Soon after hitting the Send button, he wished he hadn't gone that low, but he knew that his competitor was aggressive and would shortly outbid him. Wrong! The next message on his screen made his heart sink. It said, "No bid!" Barry had won his first online auction.

Unfortunately, approximately ten months to the day of "winning" the bid, Barry was forced to file for bankruptcy protection under Chapter 11. Not only did he lose money on every job for this new customer, but he had failed to read the small print on the bidding instructions and was responsible for the shipping charges on every job! The shipping charges alone added a minimum of 7 percent to each order. If that wasn't bad enough, because the new customer took so much of his time, he lost most of his local customers due to lack of attention.

Barry isn't the only person who has been hurt by online reverse auctions. There are a lot of misconceptions about online reverse auctions, what they are, how they work, and whether suppliers should be involved in them. One supplier told us, "Reverse auctions are like sin—if everyone is so against it, how come there's so much of it going on?" Great question! Let's take a look at what they are and what salespeople need to know about them.

What's an Online Auction?

We like this definition the best: an online reverse auction is an Internet-based bidding event with a fixed deadline, hosted by a single buyer, in which multiple suppliers compete for business. Often (not always), during the rounds of bidding, competitors can see one another's bids, though they do not know the identities of specific bidders. In many cases, the lowest bid is selected. If you have ever wondered why they call it a reverse auction, the reason is that a reverse auction is one in which the buyer rather than the seller is in control of the auction process. Think about a traditional auction: the seller is the one in control and can remove the product or service from the table if the bids are not to his liking. Not so in a reverse auction.

Recently the enthusiasm for this process has waned somewhat. The reality is that this kind of market works somewhat in commodities, but thankfully most of us aren't in the commodity business. Many buyers found that even though they got a low price, they didn't get the levels of service, quality, or support that they had become dependent on. In other cases they were forced to admit that the product they wanted may not have been a commodity after all.

Here's what some experts from the purchasing side say about the subject. "Fundamentally, reverse Internet auctions are a technology-assisted form of power-based bargaining," said Bob Emiliani. "It's a zero-sum purchasing tool where the buyer gains as a result of the supplier's loss and that is by design. That doesn't do anything to improve business relationships. Suppliers are forced to drop their prices quickly in a reverse auction, and it all comes out of the supplier's margin. That's going to create hard feelings. The whole process is oversold and it underdelivers. Buyers often go back to the original suppliers and more collaborative ways of managing costs."

Bob Emiliani and David Stec of the Center for Lean Business Management, LLC, are leading researchers on reverse auctions. Emiliani and Stec are former supply/commodity managers who used online reverse auctions.

We have also seen some of the same issues; in fact, some of the "winning" suppliers were so disabled by the low price of their bids that they were unwilling or unable to actually fulfill the terms of the deal. This is not a good thing for either party when it happens. As a result of some of these less-than-perfect transactions, the popularity of online reverse auctions has (thankfully) diminished considerably.

They haven't gone away completely, and they probably never will. So how are you going to respond when your client asks if you want to participate?

How to Protect Yourself!

You may have millions of dollars at stake with a large international company, and the pressure is on. If you say no, the company could do the auction without you, and you have just lost a major customer. If you say yes, you could lose most or all of your profit margin in a few hours but maybe retain the business. This unfortunate scenario is becoming increasingly common. Although we are not sitting in your chair as you have to make the decision, maybe we can help with the decision process.

If you have a branded product or service and the buyer has told you that this will be an anonymous reverse auction (where even the brand is not disclosed during the bid), you are at the lowest common denominator in sales—price! The answer has to be a resounding no. Preserving the brand is the most important thing you can do.

Now, there are always ways around problems, especially if lower-priced, lower-margined incremental sales are really important to your company. You could consider working through a distributor you trust or even buying or setting up a subsidiary and participating in the auction under the name of the subsidiary.

What if you are the incumbent, and your customer tells you that your product or service is going into a reverse auction? Again, a very difficult situation for all of us on the selling side. We recommend dropping what you are doing and getting to the people inside your customer organization who use the product or service. You need to create what we call FUD (fear, uncertainty, and doubt).

Point out the risks of a new supplier who's getting the business because it had the lowest price. Ask your client questions about how this might affect her job and the company's reputation for quality (remember, at this point the winner is an unkown bidder).

This reminds us of the astronaut who, when asked what he thought about right before the rockets fired to thrust him into space, said, "I'm being hurled into space by thousands of parts that were made by the low bidder!" Talk about FUD!

After the FUD factor has been implemented, sit down with the key decision makers of your company, and decide if you are going to bid. Typically when you say you will participate, you are transferring some power to the buyer through the inference that your product or service can be treated as a commodity. In some cases, as in our branding example, this could be a strategic error. Again, we would typically try to use a distributor or subsidiary or "just say no!"

If you decide to bid, you must clearly have a strategy in the bidding: where to begin and where to end. In these reverse auctions, entering without a walkaway strategy is truly a major mistake and could cause you to create a bad deal. There are too many stories about suppliers who make bad deals and then try to change the service level, or cut corners in some other way only to eventually destroy the relationship with the customer. In these cases, it truly would have been better for everyone up front to say, "No!"

If you find yourself as a potential new supplier with a chance to get some business through a reverse auction, again we recommend great caution. The incumbent can at least use FUD and other strategies to delay, change, or eliminate the auction; a new supplier who hasn't established any relationships or created any value for the customer can hope to win only through the lowest price. Again, the same internal decisions must be made, and the same walkaway strategy must be in place. Use a little caution here, particularly if anyone in your company thinks that he can get the business now and then create value and raise margins and price over time. If you start as a commodity, your chances of changing that perception over time are pretty slim.

Procurement's role in any auction is to "commoditize" all suppliers. A buyer at a major consumer products company recently told one of the authors (who was negotiating for a client), "Look, our engineers have chosen three potential suppliers for this job. As far as I am concerned, if they have been picked, it means that any one of the three companies can do the job. My job now is to get the best price. Period."

Every company has a unique value proposition for its products and services. You have to convince your clients of the inherent differences and competitive advantages of doing business with you. If the client insists on commoditizing your product, you haven't convinced her (or she is pretending you haven't convinced her) that you are, in fact, different, and that she needs the benefits only you can provide.

The momentum that reverse auctions had a few years ago is waning. This is especially true in noncommodity products and services. Until they are gone for good, however, you need to constantly differentiate yourself from the competition and sell value. If you do have to participate in a reverse auction, then please, please, have a strategy for when to stop. Otherwise, you can win the business and lose the customer or create huge holes in margin contribution.

CHAPTER 17

TYING IT ALL TOGETHER

So that's it. We've given you all the tools you need to be a great negotiator. The next part is up to you. If you aren't careful, this will be like one of those motivational speeches that gets you pumped up for a couple of days and then fades away into vague memories.

You aren't going to let that happen, are you? This is way too important. If you use these skill sets regularly, we've already shown that they will make (or save) you money. In addition, they will make your negotiations go more smoothly. And remember, since salespeople are buyers as well, you can use them in your personal life just as often as in your business deals. An example:

Last spring, Tom had a nice lunch out with his wife. After lunch, they stopped by one of those hearth and patio stores to consider the purchase of an umbrella for their deck. As they were walking around the store, they noticed a very nice set of deck furniture on display. Because the set was last year's model, it had a large "Clearance" tag on it, showing a huge price reduction. In addition to the clearance price, there was another sign that read, "Extra $100 off, today only."

The author and his wife agreed that the furniture was, indeed, a good deal and would look great on their deck. At this point she said to him, "Okay, let's see what you can do to get us a good deal." When the author pointed out the obvious, that the price was already greatly reduced, his wife simply said, "Anybody can get that price. I thought that you were the hotshot negotiator." Anyone who has been married for any length of time can probably identify with the author's (face-saving) situation. "Okay," he said, "I'll see what I can do."

At this point the salesperson strolled up and said, "Well, folks, what do you think about this patio set?" The conversation then went something like this:

Tom: It's very nice and we would love to buy it, but there's a problem.

Salesperson: Problem?

Tom: Yes. See, we came in to buy an umbrella, and if we spend all of our money on this lovely patio set, we still don't have an umbrella.

Salesperson: I see.

Tom: Now, if you could throw in [nibble] the umbrella, then maybe we could make a deal.

Salesperson: We couldn't possibly do that! These umbrellas are already value priced, and we make very little on them as it is. The furniture is marked down to rock bottom, so we have no room left to negotiate on that either.

Tom: I see. Well, how about this? If we buy the furniture and the umbrella, we'll need one of those $80 stands for the umbrella.

How about throwing that in at no charge [nibble]?

Salesperson: Ummmmmm. Okay.

Tom: And I'll need a cover for the furniture [another nibble]. How about throwing that in as well?

Salesperson: No, sir. We couldn't possibly do that! We have already given up as much as we can here.

Tom: I see. Well, how about this? Sell me the cover at half price. That's about what you really paid for it. That way, I get a good deal, and it doesn't cost you anything [split the difference].

Salesperson: Uhhhhhhhh. Okay.

Tom: I think that we are getting close to a deal here. This does include free delivery, right [another nibble]?

Salesperson: I don't know . . .

Tom: I'm sorry, but my wife has an appointment to get her hair cut in ten minutes. If we can't come to an agreement now, we'll have to leave [time pressure].

Salesperson: Okay. I guess we can deliver the furniture.

Tom: How about tomorrow?

Salesperson: Uhhh. Okay.

Tom: Just one more thing. I'm not very handy with tools so your people will set this stuff up for us, right [one last nibble]?

Salesperson (resignedly): Sure, why not?

Tom: Then we've got a deal. [Handshakes all around]

Moments later, outside the store:

Tom: Well, how'd I do?

Wife: Oh, I guess you did okay.

The issue at hand is not that you are going to impress your spouse. Fat chance. The point is that we all have lots of opportunities to practice our negotiating skills inside and outside the work environment. The more you practice, the better you get, the more money you save, and the easier your negotiations become.

One secret to successful negotiations is that you have to ask. Quite often, you may assume that things are not negotiable when, in fact, they are. The only way that you will ever know is to ask. What's the worst thing that can happen? They say no. Big deal.

Let's examine an example of the downside of the failure to negotiate effectively. In one of our classes, a participant related the story of a salary negotiation when he was joining a new company:

Company president: We'd like very much for you to join our company. How much are you looking for in salary?

Candidate: $XXXXXX [whatever he said].

Company president: It's a deal.

Not much of a negotiation, was it? Our candidate has spent the last five years kicking himself for going first in the negotiation. He will never know how much his employer might have been willing to pay him to take the job.

> ➤ PROFESSIONAL NEGOTIATING TIP
>
> It almost always is better to let the other side make the first offer. If it is higher than you expected, you can adjust your sights upward. If it is lower than what you want, you will be using the skill sets covered in this book to get to where you want to be.

To avoid this kind of situation, you are going to take steps to make sure this training stays with you. Here's what you are going to do:

Practice

Like any other skill set, your ability to negotiate will improve the more you practice it, and it will atrophy if you don't use it. Look for opportunities to negotiate in your personal life: in stores, with repairmen, with your relatives, and with others. Have fun with it! Properly done, these negotiations aren't confrontational, but a good-natured give-and-take.

Use the tools in this book:

+ Keep the Negotiation Planning Worksheet handy, and use it regularly.
+ Remember to use our techniques for keeping your emotions in check, for getting and keeping power.
+ Watch for nonverbals, and respond accordingly when you see them.
+ Read the other party's style, and adjust your style accordingly.
+ Take breaks when things aren't going the way you want them to go.
+ Have your walkaway number written down. It will keep you from doing something stupid.
+ And so on. Everything that you need to be a great negotiator is in here. All you need to do is commit it to memory and use it until it becomes second nature.

Assume That Everything Is Negotiable

Again, remember that even though you are a professional sales person, there will be times in your life when you will become "the buyer."

Therefore, until you hear otherwise, assume that just about everything is negotiable, and approach each potential negotiating situation as an opportunity to not only hone your craft but to also make, or save, a few bucks in the process.

You may be surprised at how easy this is. Contrary to what you may think, most people are not offended or annoyed when asked to negotiate. If they are interested in making a deal, they are usually perfectly willing to explore alternative ways to make it happen. If you are polite and pleasant, most people will respond to you in the same manner.

Another real-world example of a negotiation opportunity that wasn't immediately obvious:

Last spring, Tom, one of the authors, spent several hours assembling a fancy new stainless-steel gas grill. Imagine his irritation when the brand-new, state-of-the-art electronic igniter failed to light the propane. Fortunately for Tom, the company had put an 800 number right on the faceplate of the grill.

After checking the battery to be sure it wasn't the problem, Tom called the grill manufacturer's consumer hotline. The conversation went something like this:

> *Customer service rep:* XYZ Grills. How can I help you?
>
> *Tom:* My brand-new grill, model #XXX, won't light.
>
> *Rep:* Yes, sir, we are having problems with the ignition unit on that model, and we'll have to send you a new one.
>
> *Tom:* That's odd. The salesperson at the store didn't say anything about a problem with these grills.
>
> *Rep:* Well, sir, we've been having problems for a while with them. In fact, the part is on back order, and we'll have to send you one when they come in.
>
> *Tom:* I see.

Now, at this point, a lot of people would (a) yell and scream at the rep about the lousy product, or (b) meekly give the rep a mailing address and hang up. Neither is the approach that trained negotiators would take. We would see this as an opportunity to practice our negotiating skills. Here's what actually happened:

Tom: Well, then, what is your company going to do for me?

Rep: I beg your pardon? [It was clear that she'd had this conversation many times, and this was the first time that anyone had ever asked her for anything.]

Tom: Well, I have obviously bought a product with problems. It's all assembled now, so it would be difficult for me to return it.

Rep: Yes, sir.

Tom: I'm going to have to manually light the thing until you send me the part, and then I am going to have to install the igniter myself. Is that correct?

Rep: Yes, sir.

Tom: Then I think that your company ought to do something for me to compensate me for the aggravation and extra work.

Rep (perplexed, but not angry): What would you like us to do?

Tom: Well, I was thinking about buying a grill cover. I think that you ought to send me one at no charge [classic nibble].

Rep: All right. [Clearly she hadn't read our book, so she didn't make this a condition of closing the deal—so, she got another nibble.]

Tom: And a can of that expensive stainless-steel cleaner that I saw in the store. I think you should send me one of those too.

Rep: Yes, sir. We can do that.

Tom: [Fortunately for the rep, at this point he ran out of things to ask for.] Thank you.

Rep: Thank you, sir.

You are presented with countless opportunities to hone your negotiating skills. You need to recognize and seize these opportunities because they provide you with invaluable practice time. Not only that, you would be amazed at the deals you can get just by asking.

Remember, price isn't the only issue in most negotiations. If it turns out that the price isn't negotiable, look for opportunities to influence terms or other aspects of the deal.

Enjoy It When You Get to Be the Customer

As a salesperson, you don't get to be the customer very often. When you do, you should make the most of it. When it's your turn to buy a car, an appliance, or whatever, you should use all of the techniques described in this book to make sure that you get the best possible deals for yourself.

You will more than recoup the price of this book the first time you need to buy a major appliance if you apply the principles we have been discussing. Plus, you will have fun. All of the pressure is going to be on the seller, not you.

Take Pride in Your New Skills

Quite often, we will begin a workshop by asking for a show of hands of people who negotiate every day. Generally everyone in the class will raise a hand. We follow up by asking, "Who here feels that they are good negotiators?" It is rare to get more than one or two hands.

The fact is that most of us, including some very successful businesspeople, feel that we've got a lot of room for improvement when it comes to our negotiating ability.

By absorbing and practicing the content from this book, you will become much more confident and assured in the many negotiations that you will face from here on out. Everything that we have covered is ethical, aboveboard, and professional, so you needn't have any reservations about using these techniques.

Now, if you are up for it, we've got one more challenge for you. This is just to make sure that you have really absorbed what we've put in this book. Go to the next chapter and take the quiz. Your results will give you a good idea of where you stand as a negotiator.

CHAPTER 18

TESTING YOUR KNOWLEDGE (ARE YOU REALLY READY TO FACE THOSE BUYERS?)

THINK YOU ARE READY TO GO OUT AND PLAY WITH THE BIG boys? Let's find out. In this chapter, we'll give you twenty opportunities to test your new negotiation skills. It is a no-fault way to practice before you get in front of your customers.

We'll give you a scenario and then multiple choices for how to handle it. You can find answers and a grading scale in Appendix II. No looking ahead or peeking at the answers. Good luck!

Scenario #1

Your client is discussing your proposal relative to those of your competitors. As she is talking, you notice that she is touching the lower part of her face. She states that you are at least 20 percent higher than the other offers. The correct reaction to this is to

(a) ask her for more time so that you can resubmit your proposal with revised numbers based on this new information.

(b) tell her that your offer is the best that you can do.

(c) ask her to tell you more about the competitive offers.

(d) tell her that you will drop your price by 20 percent if that will close the deal.

Scenario #2

As you open discussions on a new project with your client, he brings up a product problem that occurred two years ago. He claims that the problem resulted in a $5,000 loss for the company and asks that you adjust your quote by that amount to "make them whole" on the earlier problem. The correct response is to

(a) see if he will split the difference and settle for $2,500.

(b) tell him that both sides had a hand in that problem and his company was just as responsible for it as your company.

(c) tell him that you don't know anything about it and you'll have to get back to him on it.

(d) acknowledge that the problem occurred, agree to revisit it, but set it aside until this deal is concluded.

Scenario #3

At the end of a negotiation, the client asks you for a concession. What she is asking for is relatively unimportant and of low value to you. You know that giving her what she wants will help you get the deal. You decide to

(a) agree to give her what she asks for in order to move the deal along.

(b) agree to the request if the client will agree to something of roughly equal value in return.

(c) just say no.

(d) think it over by taking a break.

Scenario #4

Throughout an important negotiation, the opposing team leader has come across as a strong C1 (conquer) style. You are leading your team, and all your efforts have failed to be more collaborative. The best style for you to adopt now is

(a) concede.

(b) collaborate.

(c) conquer.

(d) compromise.

Scenario #5

During an intense one-on-one negotiation session, the buyer surprises you with a lowball offer from a previously unknown competitor. This new information upsets your carefully crafted presentation, and you are unsure how to proceed. At this point, you should

(a) go ahead with your presentation as planned and hope for the best.

(b) tell the buyer that you need to make a phone call and excuse yourself.

(c) stop your presentation and discuss the lowball offer.

(d) tell the buyer that you need to "run down the hall."

Scenario #6

Your meeting is going along as planned, but suddenly the buyer digs in his heels on a relatively minor point. His position makes no sense to you. You should

(a) ask him to help you understand why this particular point is so important.

(b) tell him he's not making any sense.

(c) try to get him to see things from your point of view.

(d) take a break.

Scenario #7

The buyer asks to look at your proposal. She picks it up, flips to the last page (the one with the numbers), and looks at the prices. After a brief moment, she sighs deeply and puts her head in her hand. You should

(a) go back to your value proposition and resell her.

(b) tell her that this is just a preliminary quote and you can do better.

(c) ask her what she doesn't like about it.

(d) do nothing.

Scenario #8

You are at what should be the final meeting to close a big deal with an important client. As the players from both sides come in and take their seats, you notice that your buyer's boss, who has taken an active role in the deal so far, isn't in the room. You decide to

(a) try to get a quick sign-off on the deal before the boss shows up.

(b) offer to come back later.

(c) ask the buyer why his boss isn't there.

(d) not put your best offer on the table.

Scenario #9

As you are presenting your proposal, you notice that the buyer is touching his fingertips together in front of him. The correct response is to

(a) keep going; he's really into it.

(b) stop talking and ask him what he thinks of the proposal so far.

(c) take a break.

(d) give him more details.

Scenario #10

As you plan for an important negotiation, you know that price is going to be a critical factor. You know that you need to plot out your pricing strategy in advance. As you begin to formulate your plan, the first number that you need to know is

(a) what you think it will take to get the deal.

(b) your starting price.

(c) your walkaway price.

(d) your first move.

Scenario #11

After a particularly long and complex negotiation, you finally get the client to sign the deal. You can hardly believe that it is over. Your next move is to

(a) get out of her office quickly before she changes something.

(b) call a meeting of your internal team.

(c) offer to take the client to dinner to celebrate.

(d) formulate a simple action plan together.

Scenario #12

You are planning for an important client meeting. You find out that in addition to the buyer, the other team is bringing two subject matter experts (SMEs) and the corporate counsel. In thinking about your own team you decide to

(a) go it alone because you know that you can handle anything that comes up.

(b) bring along four or five SMEs of your own so that you can deal with anything that might pop up.

(c) bring two SMEs to balance theirs and your own lawyer.

(d) bring a senior manager from your company in case the client wants a decision that you don't have the authority to make.

Scenario #13

It is the same as #12 except that you find out that your legal person can't make the meeting. You should

(a) go with the team you've got.

(b) reschedule the meeting so that you can bring your lawyer.

(c) get an internal briefing from your lawyer before attending the meeting.

(d) don't talk directly to their attorney and take notes.

Scenario #14

The client studies your proposal for several minutes, looks up, and says, "Your competitor has a better offer, so what are you going to do?" You respond by saying:

(a) "How much better do I have to do?"

(b) "This is just a preliminary quote."

(c) "Tell me more about the competitive offer."

(d) "It's the best that we can do. Hopefully it will win the deal."

Scenario #15

Which of the following items is typically not an equal business standing issue?

(a) Dressing appropriately

(b) Confidence

(c) Your title

(d) Your badge placement

Scenario #16

The buyer says to you, "Congratulations, we have decided to award your company parts (1) and (2) of the contract. Your prices were very good. We are going to give your competitors parts (3) through (6)." You had intentionally reduced your margins on (1) and (2) in order to get (3) through (6). Now what are you going to do?

(a) Sign the deal as quickly as possible.

(b) Say that he can't have (1) and (2) unless he gives you
    (3) through (6).

(c) Take a break.

(d) Tell him that you will need to refigure the prices for (1) and (2) only.

Scenario #17

You are deadlocked with the buyer over the price of your product. Time is running short. The buyer looks at you and says, "Why don't we just split the difference?" You look at the numbers and realize that if you meet her halfway, the result is a good deal for your company. You say,

(a) "Okay."

(b) "I'll have to make a phone call."

(c) "If I agree to that, can we sign the contract now?"

(d) None of the above.

Scenario #18

As you are working up the numbers for an important client presentation, you are strategizing on your opening price point. Your walkaway price is $8,000, and your starting point needs to be approximately $2,000 higher. Which price point below would be the most appropriate?

(a) $10,000

(b) $9,995

(c) $10,185

(d) None of the above

Scenario #19

You walk into the client's conference room for an important meeting with the client's product acquisition team. The room itself is right off the senior VP's office. Your team has arrived early, and you've got your choice of seating. You are the lead negotiator. Based on this chart, which seat do you choose for yourself?

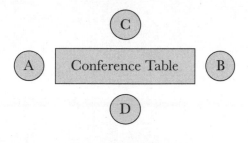

Senior VP's Office

(a) A

(b) B

(c) C

(d) D

Scenario #20

You are sitting in your car in traffic. Your cell phone rings, and it's the buyer for a big deal that you have been working on for a month. The buyer says, "I'm glad I caught you. We are going into a meeting now to make a decision on your deal. I need your best and final offer now!" Your answer is:

(a) "You already have our best offer."

(b) "Give me ten minutes to review your file and I'll call you back."

(c) "How do my prices stack up against the competition's?"

(d) "Hello! Hello! You are cutting out on me and I can't hear you. I'll have to call you back."

Now go find the answers in Appendix II. How did you do?

CHAPTER 19

CAR BUYING: FINALLY YOU GET TO BE THE CUSTOMER!

IT IS IMPOSSIBLE TO CONDUCT A NEGOTIATIONS WORKSHOP in North America and not end up talking about the new-car buying experience. This seems to be a universally unpopular activity regardless of the buyer's age, background, or social status. Some people are so traumatized by the process that they actually hire other people to buy their cars for them!

It doesn't have to be this way. As in an earlier chapter, this is one of those rare cases where we are the buyers, not the sellers. If you think about it, we should be the ones with all the power in a transaction like this. After all,

+ it's our money, and a lot of it at that!
+ we don't have to buy a car from any particular dealer.
+ they need us a lot more than we need them.

Unfortunately the car buying process has evolved into a complicated ritual, pitting the seller against the buyer in an environment in which all the odds are stacked against the buyer. This isn't because car dealers are evil or immoral people. They are not. But they operate in a difficult marketplace in which they have to maximize their profits on every single vehicle that they sell in order to survive.

That's their job. Not yours. Yours is to negotiate the best deal for yourself that you can.

In this chapter, we will show you how to turn the tables on our friends the car dealers and use your own set of tactics to get and hold the power in this negotiation. If you do it properly, not only will you get a great deal for yourself, but it will be the most efficient and painless car buying process you have ever experienced.

Not only that, but virtually all of the negotiations can be done over the phone. The only time that you will have to leave home is to sign the papers and pick up your car! No driving all over town. No bad coffee. No hanging around the salesperson's cubicle waiting for a counteroffer.

One tactic of car dealers is to keep you on their property as long as possible. They know that the more time you have tied up with them, the less likely you are to go somewhere else and start the same process all over again. You're not going to play their game, however. You are going to make them play yours.

Part One: How to Buy a Car Over the Phone

Step #1: Decide What You Want to Buy (You Probably Can't Do This Part Over the Phone)

This is not a book on how to choose a car. You need to do that on your own. Talk to your friends. Read *Consumer Reports*. Read the car buff magazines. Find whatever meets your needs. Then drive some cars and check the prices and decide on what you want. Make it clear to the car salespersons at the dealerships that you are just looking around and that you are not ready to buy. This is important: regardless of what you tell them, they will pressure you to buy. Do not, under any circumstances, fall in love with a particular car at this point! You will get clobbered. Now you need to decide on the following:

+ make and model of the vehicle
+ interior and exterior colors
+ optional equipment

The more narrowly you focus on the exact package that you want, the better this system works.

Step #2: Go Online and Do Your Research

Now that you know exactly what you want, the vehicle becomes a commodity. You don't really care where you buy it at this point, as long as you get a good deal.

Go to www.edmunds.com or www.kbb.com, and get the financial information on the model that you have selected. You want to know

+ dealer invoice with the options that you want.
+ destination charges.
+ dealer list price.
+ TMV (target market value): This is an average of what other purchasers have been actually paying for the vehicle. If you see a big spread between list and TMV, it tells you that dealers are readily discounting. A small spread means that particular model is hot, and the dealers don't feel they have to give up much on price. (Note: If

a vehicle is really hot [like Mini Coopers and hybrid vehicles in 2004–5, for example], there may be no opportunity to discount. In this very rare case, about all you ask for are freebies like floor mats.)

+ dealer incentives, rebates, etc., offered by the manufacturer.

+ the value of your trade-in. Based on your mileage and the condition of your vehicle, you will be able to get a realistic feel for wholesale and retail for your car.

It might be tempting to try some of the pop-up car buying services that will appear while you are online. We recommend that you ignore them. They may get you a car, but they won't get you the best deal, and they can be slow to respond.

Step #3: Set Up a Spreadsheet

Things are about to get busy, so you will need to stay organized. To get the best deal, you need to have multiple dealers bidding for your business. Remember, in any negotiation, alternatives are the source of real power. You will have lots of them. To keep it all straight, you need a spreadsheet.

You will need to keep track of which dealerships you have contacted, whom you spoke with and when, what the offer is, and other notes about freebies and nibbles (more on that later). See the sample spreadsheet in Appendix III.

Step #4: Research the Dealers

With your spreadsheet open, go back online to the Web site of the manufacturer of the vehicle that you want. Usually it is www.[nameof-manufacturer].com.

When you get there, go to the "Dealer Locator" section and ask for a list of dealers within a 150-mile range. Enter the names, street addresses, and phone numbers of these dealers on your spreadsheet.

You may get offers to put you in e-mail contact with these dealers while you are on the manufacturer's Web site. Ignore them. No dealer is going to negotiate seriously via e-mail with someone he doesn't know is for real.

Get a fresh cup of coffee and take a deep breath, because you are about to start negotiating. This is the fun part!

Step #5: Call Dealers

Pick the dealer that is at the outside limit of your geographical comfort zone, and give it a call. A small-town dealer isn't a bad place to start; after all, you are just warming up.

Note: Weekends are bad times to call. Dealerships are busy, phones are ringing, and customers are standing around. The best time is a weekday morning when the salespeople are sitting around with nothing to do, wondering where their next deal is going to come from.

When the operator answers, ask to speak to a salesperson. When that person picks up, say something like this: "Good morning. My name is xxxxxx. I have decided to buy a [your color, your make and model] with [your options]. Have you got one in stock?"

The salesperson will say, "Yes," "We can get one," or "We have something close." She will probably suggest that you come in for a testdrive or start a sales pitch on what a wonderful selection you have made. Don't listen.

Tell her that you have already had the sales pitch and the test-drive. Say, "Look, I have already made up my mind to buy the car. I am shopping for the best deal. I live in [your town], but I don't mind driving to [wherever the dealer is] if the price is right. Before you quote me a price, there are a few things we need to be clear on, just so that we don't waste each other's time." And then you make the following points clear:

+ "I don't want any equipment or add-ons that I haven't asked for, no paint protection packages, no wheel locks, and so forth."

+ "I am not going to pay any ADP [additional dealer profit] or market adjustment fees." (These are just added profit for the dealer.)

+ "I am not paying any kind of processing fee." (She may say that all transactions carry a fee. You say, "That's fine; just include it in my net cost. But I will be comparing your price to the other offers that I receive.")

+ "I don't want any surprises. Just give me the net price on the vehicle, and let me know what taxes and title cost will be."

+ "I am going to buy the car in the next three days. It will be a cash deal with no trade-in." (Note: You may want to finance it and you may want to trade in your old car, but now is not the time to bring up these issues. Doing that will just muddy the water. What you are trying to get at is the "real" net price at which the dealer is willing to sell you the vehicle.)

That conversation shouldn't take more than five minutes. But you have told the salesperson that (a) you are a serious (indeed hot!) prospect, (b) you aren't going to waste a lot of her time with the sales stuff, and (c) you want a bottom-line price.

You have also told her that you know about all the extra income ploys and you aren't going to play that game. If she says that all of their vehicles come with the $350 paint protection package, for example, you say that you don't place any value on it (it's just wax), and you won't pay any more for a vehicle with or without it.

She will say that she needs to talk to the manager to get a price for you. Tell her that's fine, give her your number, and ask her to call you back when she has it. Don't let her put you on hold and wait. That's playing her game. Remind her of your tight time frame, thank her, and hang up.

Enter her name next to the dealership on your spreadsheet.

Now call another four or five dealers on the list, gradually working your way closer to home or into the larger cities.

Do not call your local dealer(s) yet. That doesn't happen until step #9.

Enter all of the contact information onto your spreadsheet, get another cup of coffee, and wait for the callbacks.

Step #6: Wait for Callbacks

Things start moving quickly now, so have your spreadsheet handy.

As the salespeople (or sometimes the sales managers) start calling back with prices, you need to stay focused on the net price of exactly the vehicle that you want. Don't let them try to trade you up or add on options that you don't need.

Make it clear that you are shopping for the best "out the door" (everything included) price and that you will be talking to other dealers.

When they quote you a price, enter it on your spreadsheet, but make sure that it really is the price. Ask the salesperson again, "Are there any other expenses that will pop up when we go to close this deal? How much are title and taxes? What is the total bottom-line figure?"

Once you are sure that you have all of the information, thank them and tell them that you will be in touch.

Who has the power in this negotiation? You do!

Repeat this process as the other dealers call you back.

Step #7: Analyze the Data and Follow Up

Once you have heard from all of the out-of-town dealers, it should be fairly easy to pick the two or three best deals. Make sure that you are comparing apples to apples. You need to assign some value to your travel time; that is, you aren't going to drive 300 miles to save $20, but you might as well drive 120 miles to save $800.

Call back the two or three dealers with the best prices, and let them know that you are interested in buying from them, but that they "need to do better" in order to win your business. When they ask you "how much better" (and they will), don't tell them, but let them know that you are close to deciding and they need to get their best offer on the table.

Call the dealers with the higher offers, and let them know that you are removing them from consideration because their prices weren't competitive. This will encourage them to sharpen their pencils or at least get them to stop calling you.

Be sure to update your spreadsheet as the offers change.

Who's got the power? You!

Who's feeling the pressure? They are.

At this point, you shouldn't have more than an hour invested in the deal.

Do a reality check by comparing what you've got so far with the TMV figure from your research.

Note on TMV numbers: TMV numbers are useful in establishing a baseline, but the information may be dated or inaccurate. One of the authors recently bought one vehicle for $1,700 below TMV and another for $3,000 below TMV. Just because other people are paying too much for their cars doesn't mean that you should.

Step #8: Enter Final Negotiations

Call the two dealers with the best offers, and tell them that they are close but not quite there. Start with the one with the lowest price. Give him one more chance, and tell him you are going to make a decision in the next thirty minutes. If he says you have his best price, then it is time to nibble. Have a list handy of little things that he could throw in:

+ floor mats
+ a trunk mat
+ wheel locks
+ luggage rack
+ tank of gas

You get the idea. If (when) he throws in an item, move down the list, and ask for another until he quits or you run out of nibbles.

Go back to the dealer with the second-lowest offer, and give her a chance to beat the other guy. If she can, great. Tell her that you think you have a deal, but you need to think it over for a little while. If she is still high, tell her so and see what happens.

At this point, the dealers may ask to see copies of the competitive bids. Tell them that you won't do that (just as you wouldn't show their offer to anyone else) but that you are sure they are legitimate.

Note: Before you hang up with both of these dealerships, make them go over the figures one more time to be sure that there are no hidden costs or surprises.

You can even say something like this: "Just so I'm sure that we understand each other here, I am planning to walk into your dealership with a check made out for exactly $xxxxx and walk out with the keys to this car, right? I don't want to drive all the way to [wherever] for nothing."

If you are not confident that the above will happen, ask them to put the sales manager or owner on the phone to confirm the deal.

You can ask them to fax you a copy of the offer, but don't be surprised if they won't. They don't want you showing their deals to other dealers if they are really low.

Update your spreadsheet. Grab a cup of decaf, and get ready to make one more call.

Step #9: Contact the Local Dealer

At this point you should be looking at a great deal. Call your local dealer, and ask for the salesperson who took you on the test-drive and gave you the sales pitch back when you were shopping.

When he picks up, say something like this: "Good news, Bob. I have decided to buy that [Glitzmobile III] that you showed me last week. I have been checking prices, and I have a quote from another dealer. If you can meet or beat the price, I will come in tomorrow and pick up the car." Tell him exactly what your best offer is.

Bob will be very suspicious of the price because it is so low. He may ask you to come in to talk about it. He may ask you to identify the other dealer or to bring in a copy of the offer in writing. Tell Bob that you aren't going to do that, but that you are sure the offer is valid.

Ask him to talk it over with his sales manager and get back to you. Tell him you need an answer quickly because you need to get back to the other dealer.

While you are waiting, calculate exactly what it is worth to you not to have to drive xxx miles out of town to buy the car.

When Bob calls you back, one of several things will happen. If he meets or beats your best offer, try a couple more nibbles, and then tell him he has a deal. Reconfirm the total price one more time, then set up a time to pick up your new car. If he is high, even after adjusting for travel, thank him for his time, and tell him that he'll get your service business (if the winning dealer is out of town).

Call the low bidder, and tell him that you are very close to pulling the trigger. Ask for one more nibble, then agree to do the deal, and arrange a time to pick up your new car.

Step #10: Sign the Deal

Show up at the appointed time, and do the deal. Don't let the salesperson talk you into any last-minute add-ons, extended warranties, or whatever. Shake hands with everyone. Smile. Get checked out on your new car, and leave.

If any surprises pop up (not likely at this point), stop the negotiations immediately, get up, and walk out. Call the next dealer on your list, and buy the car there. Notify the manufacturer of your bad experience.

Part Two: If You Decide to Buy in Person

If for some reason (maybe you need a used car) you decide to buy your car in person, the basics remain the same, but you need to watch out for some new traps. We recommend this only for people who really enjoy the negotiating process. Remember, you are going to be playing on their turf, and they get a lot more practice than you do.

Do your homework (see above), and have your walkaway price written down and in your pocket before you set foot in the showroom.

Go on a weekday when things are slow so that you'll get plenty of attention.

Let them know that you are ready to buy and don't need a sales pitch. Let them know that you have been calling around for prices.

Here are some tactics that you will probably experience:

+ Time pressure. The longer they can keep you there, the less likely you are to go somewhere else to start the whole unpleasant process over again.

Countertactic: Tell them that you have only thirty minutes before another appointment and that you will leave if you can't reach an agreement. If they stall anyway, get up and head for the door.

✦ Bundling. They will probably want to discuss your trade-in and financing options. This muddies the water on the actual price of the vehicle.

Countertactic: Tell them that you want to discuss only the cash price for the vehicle.

✦ Higher authority. You knew this was coming! The salesperson says that he has to run your offer by the boss. Since he is planning to be gone awhile, it fits nicely with the time-pressure tactic (see above).

Countertactic: Tell the salesperson that you want to deal directly with the decision maker (sales manager, general manager, or whomever). If he says that person is too busy, you reply, "No problem." Then write your phone number down, and say, "Have him call me when he is not too busy." And head for the door. We guarantee that you will meet the boss before you get very far.

You are not going to fall for the salesperson's tactics, and you are going to turn the tables on her with some tricks of your own. Here are some tactics (see Chapter 5) that you will want to use:

✦ The squeeze. Look at the first offer and say, "You'll have to do better than that." If she asks, "How much better?" she has taken the bait! Throw out a lowball figure and let the games begin.

✦ The flinch. When she makes a counteroffer, look at it, groan, and wait for her to jump in and try to make you feel better with a concession.

+ Red herrings. If the vehicle has a weak point (low gas mileage, below-average safety ratings, so-so resale value), bring it up as a concern. If you are equally interested in a competitive model from another manufacturer, let the salesperson know.

+ The bogey. Tell her you can afford to pay only xxx for your new car.

+ Split the difference. Offer to split the difference between her price and your offer. If she does it, go for it, change the subject, redirect the negotiation to another, nonprice area, then circle back around and see if you can get her to split the difference again.

+ Higher authority. If you have her best deal and want to buy some time to think about it, tell her that you need to run everything by your significant other.

+ The nibble. Make a list before you leave home. Once the price is as low as it is going to go, start asking for extras: floor mats, wheel locks, roof rack, whatever. If she says yes to one, ask for another. See how far down your list you can get.

If you feel yourself getting emotional or losing power, take a break. If you brought someone with you, don't discuss your strategy with him in the showroom (go outside so you can talk in private).

Always remember that you are the buyer. You have the power. And you are ready to walk away if you can't get the deal that you want!

How to See Through "Factory Deals"

In this era of subsidized interest rates and "employee pricing" programs, it is tempting to assume that the advertised price on a vehicle is the best price. This isn't necessarily so. The factory deal quite often doesn't affect the dealer margin. Once you have identified the impact of the manufacturer deals on the price, then you want to ask the dealer what he is going to do to sweeten the deal.

Financing

Dealers make money on the spread between their rate and what you are charged. If you need financing, it is generally cheaper to arrange it up front on your own. The dealer will be happy to finance your vehicle for you, and it shouldn't affect your deal at all if you bring it up at the last minute. It is always a good idea to run a credit check on yourself and make sure that the report is correct before you talk to anyone about a loan.

Trade-In

If you have a car that you want to trade, you have several choices. The main thing is to keep the trade separate from the new car because dealers can really muddy the water if you tie them together. If your car is more than a few years old, the dealer probably doesn't want it on the lot. The dealer may have a wholesaler on hand to look at it and make you an offer. It will be low.

You can get an offer from a place like CarMax. It will be low. Do this before you go to the dealership so you have something to compare the dealer's offer to.

Dealerships make a lot of money by buying used cars cheaply, cleaning them up, and reselling them. You can do the same. If you absolutely want no part in selling your car yourself, then wholesale it.

If every dollar is crucial, however, spend a few bucks and get your car detailed and put a sign in the window. If no one has shown any interest in it after a few days, then put it in the newspaper. You can base your asking price on the figure that you got from Edmunds (retail), or you can go online and look at what similar cars are going for in private (not dealer) sales. Lots of used cars are sold on eBay. Yours might sell there too.

Use the skill sets from this book to negotiate with prospective buyers. Use the wholesale offer as your reality check.

Used Cars

Used cars fall into a gray area between commodities and unique items. For example, if you are trying to buy a vintage Bugatti and there are only five examples in existence, you don't have many alternatives; hence, you don't have much negotiating leverage.

If you are interested in a 2002 Ford Taurus, however, of which there are countless thousands roaming our streets, you have a much stronger bargaining position. The key here is to research the current market prices (online, your newspaper, dealer lots, etc.) and to know as much as possible about the condition of the particular vehicle that you are considering. If you are not mechanically inclined, it might be well worth it to pay a good mechanic to do an inspection before making an offer.

Also, before beginning the negotiations, plan your moves (Chapter 9), and always, always, always have a walkaway price written down.

Final Comment

Car dealers have a tough job these days. Everyone can find out their margins, and we all have a lot more choices of how and where to buy.

Just remember that you have the power in these negotiations, and with a little planning and preparation, you can resist the various tactics they use to shift that power away from you.

You are spending a lot of money here, so you might as well have fun with it!

APPENDIX I

Negotiation Planning Worksheet

What They Want	What We Want

POSSIBLE MATCHES?

KEY AREAS OF DISCUSSION:

THEIR MEASUREMENTS?

FACE-SAVING ISSUES?

Maximum:

Starting Point:

First Move:

Second Move:

Minimum (walkaway):

ADDITIONAL ITEMS (COUNTERNIBBLES):

ALTERNATIVE STRATEGY:

APPENDIX II

Answer Key

Scenario #1

Answer (c) is correct. Remember from our chapter on nonverbals that touching the lower face is usually a sign that the other party is either unsure of what she is saying or flat-out lying? You would never make a business decision on information that you are receiving under these circumstances. You need to figure out what's going on, and the best way to do that is to ask open-ended questions such as, "Tell me more about the competitive offers."

Scenario #2

Answer (d) is correct. This is a classic red herring. The customer is trying to use an incident from the past as leverage on this deal. You need to use the "set-aside" technique in order to decouple the red herring from your current deal. Offer to revisit the red herring issue after this one has been resolved. In most cases, the red herring simply goes away.

Scenario #3

Answer (b) is correct. This is a nibble, and you know from the tactics chapter that if you give in to a nibble, you will get (surprise!) another nibble. Always be prepared with your own list of counternibbles, and ask for something of approximately equal value in return.

Scenario #4

Answer (c) is correct. If the other party is using the conquer style, you need to move into that style in order to avoid being bullied or steam-rolled. Quite often, C1's will default to a backup style that's easier to deal with when they see that the conquer style isn't getting them anywhere.

Scenario #5

When things aren't going your way, you need to do something to break the negative momentum and regroup. Taking a break (d) is the best way to accomplish this without losing face or giving up power. Answer (b) gets you out of the room to regroup, but it exposes the fact that you may need some-one else's help with this new information. In other words, you've lost power in the negotiation by showing them their tactic got the best of you.

Scenario #6

Answer (a) is correct. When a negotiation that has previously been proceeding in an orderly and rational fashion suddenly stops making sense to you, you should look for face-saving issues. If you keep pound-ing away at the other side and expect him to change his position, you are likely to waste a lot of time and frustrate both sides. Find out what the other party needs to save face, figure out a way to get it to him, and figure out what you are going to ask for in return.

Scenario #7

Answer (d) is correct. This is the flinch, essentially a fake nonverbal signal. The buyer wants you to believe that something about your pro-posal has hurt her. If you take the bait, you will jump in and offer her some kind of concession to make her feel better. Don't fall for it. Just sit there quietly, and wait for her to speak first.

Scenario #8

Answer (d) is correct. If a key decision maker suddenly goes missing, you should assume the other side is setting you up for a higher-authority tactic. When this happens, you should insist that the person join the meeting, or you should withhold something from the offer so that you can respond to the inevitable bite that he will put on you.

Scenario #9

Answer (b) is correct. He is steepling. Roughly translated, the gesture means, "I already know all about this, and I wish that you would shut up and let me talk." The best response is to stop talking and ask him a question. He wants to talk.

Scenario #10

Answer (c) is correct. When planning your pricing strategy, always start by determining your walkaway price. That's the point at which you no longer care if you get the business or not. By figuring out what this number is and writing it down, you ensure that you won't get carried away or outmaneuvered and do something stupid. This gives you power.

Scenario #11

Answer (d) is correct. It is always a good idea to take a few minutes and put together an action plan to ensure that the parties involved in making your deal happen actually do what they are supposed to do. A plan, with milestones and responsibilities spelled out, will keep people focused. It will also protect you from selective amnesia. Finally, in the event that your counterpart at the client company gets downsized, fired, or promoted, you are in a much better position with the replacement if you have a plan in place.

Scenario #12

Answer (c) is best. When putting together your team, you want to balance their side with yours. If they have SMEs, you probably need them too. Don't outnumber them, or you will send a signal that your company is top-heavy with people. Don't go it alone unless you are qualified to deal, in depth, with the SMEs.

Scenario #13

Answer (b) is best. Lawyers are a special case. You aren't qualified or authorized by your company to discuss legal matters. If the other side has an attorney and you don't, you should reschedule for a time when your counsel can make it.

Scenario #14

Answer (c) is correct. This is a classic squeeze. If you say, "How much better do I have to do?" you have taken the bait, and from that point on, you are negotiating with yourself. You are much better off to ask the client what he is comparing your offer to. Then you can look for apples/oranges situations and resell your value proposition.

Scenario #15

Answer (c) is correct. The way you dress, shake hands, and exude confidence—not your title—establishes equal business standing.

Scenario #16

Answer (d) is correct. Remember when we discussed the cherry picker in the tactics chapter? The buyer is using it on you here. Just because he has decided to pick and choose among the prospective suppliers doesn't mean you have to honor a price that was based on a bundled quote. You should let the buyer know that your prices were based on a basket of products and that you will be happy to requote the deal based on the reduced scope.

Scenario #17

Answer (c) is correct. You should always be wary when the buyer wants you to split the difference. It is often a tactic designed to get you to lower your price while the buyer pretends to be collaborative. If you aren't careful, you can get split multiple times while the buyer hasn't really moved at all. There are cases (for instance, if you run out of time to explore other solutions) when splitting the difference is the only way to get to a deal. If the result of splitting is acceptable to you in this situation, then let the other party know that you will do so only as a condition of signing the order. In this way, you avoid the trap of multiple splits or further concessions.

Scenario #18

Answer (c) is correct. Remember, round numbers invite negotiation. They look made up, rounded up, and full of fluff. An odd number, like (c), looks like it was built from the ground up and has some basis in fact, not wishful thinking. Answer (b) appears to be "retail" pricing.

Scenario #19

Answer (c) or (d) is correct. In a conference room adjoining an executive's office, the odds are very good that the executive has "his" spot in the room. The odds are also very good that it's A. If you pick A, he will be annoyed or uncomfortable. If you pick B, you will be facing him across an expanse of table in a confrontational way. C and D are better choices because they put you in a more collaborative position.

Remember that you aren't going to sit down until the other party comes in. You don't want them looking down on you; it robs you of power. Wait till they come in and shake hands, and then everyone sits down together.

Scenario #20

Answer (b) is correct. This tactic is designed to catch you off guard and panic you into shooting some kind of crazy number off the top of your head. You want to buy yourself time to gather your thoughts, review the offer, and decide on the appropriate response.

Your Score (the number you answered correctly): _____

Based on our experience, here's how you should interpret your results:

If you scored:

20–17	Super job! You are ready to negotiate in the big leagues.
16–14	Great job! You are ready to negotiate and win!
13–10	Okay. You might want to brush up on those areas where you lost points, but you are on the right track.

9–5   Reread the book before you attempt to negotiate anything more serious than a lamp at a yard sale.

4 or below   Consider hiring someone to do your negotiating for you.

APPENDIX III

Sample Car Buying Spreadsheet

Vehicle: '04 Zepher
Options: automatic, no nav., pearl white

Edmunds Data	MSRP: $32,650	Invoice: $30,300	Dest. Chg.: $545	Dealer Cost: $30,845	TMV: $31,974
Rebates/Incentives	1/9% financing				

Trade In-Edmunds	'96 Outlaw z30, 88k mi.	Wholsle: $5,421	Private: $6,600	Retail: $8,227
Offers	AutoMax: $4,700	Car Pros: $4,850	Smilin' Jack: $3,500	

Dealer	Address	Phone	Contact	Vehicle	Title	Tax	Processing	Other	Total	Avail.
City Zepher	15111 Jefferson Ave. Newport News, VA 23602	(757) 866-7060	Bob Smith	$32,000	$50	$1,024	0	0	$33,074	10-Feb
Crown Zepher	4405 W. Broad St. Richmond, VA	303-9633	Harry Jones	$31,395	$50	$1,040	$199	trunk mat mud guard wheel locks	$32,684	12-Feb
A-1 Zepher	1200 Columbia Pike Falls Church, VA 22401	(703) 888-2268	Mary Liu	$30,959	$50	$991	0	trunk mat wheel locks	$32,000	now
Lee Motors	900 Auto Park Blvd. Cary, NC 27511	(919) 512-8200	Dale Simmons	$32,000	$50	$1,024	0		$33,074	now
Capital Zepher	3911 Lee Jackson Hwy. Chantilly, VA 20151	(703) 666-6600	Tim Brown	$30,864	$50	$986	0	trunk mat	$31,450	now

BIBLIOGRAPHY

Babcock, Linda, and Sara Laschever. *Women Don't Ask*. Princeton, NJ: Princeton University Press, 2003.

Camp, Jim. *Start with No . . . The Negotiating Tools That the Pros Don't Want You to Know*. New York, NY: Crown Business, 2002.

Cohen, Herb. *You Can Negotiate Anything*. Secaucus, NJ: Bantam Books, 2003.

Dawson, Roger. *The Secrets of Power Negotiating*. Franklin Lakes, NJ: Career Press, Inc., 2001.

Fisher, Roger, and William Ury. *Getting to Yes*. New York: Penguin Books, 1991.

Haberfeld, Steven. "Government to Government Negotiations: How the Timbhisa Shoshone Got Its Land Back." *American Indian Culture and Research Journal*. Vol. 24, no. 4 (2000).

Karrass, Chester. *The Negotiating Game*. Revised edition. New York, NY: HarperCollins, 1992.

Krause, Donald G. *The Art of War for Executives*. New York, NY: Perigee Trade, 1995.

Pease, Allan. *Signals*. New York: Bantam Books, 1984.

ABOUT THE AUTHORS

Ron J. Lambert is the chairman and co-founder of Yukon Alongside Management Company based in Richmond, Virginia focuses on turning salespeople into businesspeople. Each Along Management consultant has a minimum of twenty-five years of s experience and has served at least at a vice presidential level.

Prior to founding Alongside Management in 1989, Ron directed customer relations and negotiating of major contracts for the $500 m lion Pharmaceutical Division of A. H. Robins Inc. and served as seni vice president for Data Systems Corporation.

Ron has served on the adjunct faculty of Virginia Commonwealt University as well as the University of Richmond's Management Institute and he has conducted workshops for Cornell University.

He has personally conducted more than five hundred customized negotiation workshops throughout the United States, Italy, France, South Africa, Germany, the Netherlands, the United Kingdom, Hong Kong, Canada, and Brussels.

He has helped a number of clients conduct real multimillion-dollar negotiations, serving on the negotiating team itself or acting as a senior adviser for the negotiating team of the client.

Ron has consulted with and conducted programs for many companies, including M&M MARS, Wyeth Pharmaceuticals, Nextel, Gillette,

Vistage, PepsiAmericas, GlaxoSmithKline Consumer Healthcare, BP Lubricants, EDS, Allergan, General Electric, Dominion Virginia Power, Reader's Digest, Ethyl Corporation, Swedish Match, AMF, General Medical Corporation, and ABB.

Ron lives in Mathews County, Virginia, a small community located near the Chesapeake Bay, with his wife, Debbie. Both Ron and his wife are members of the Mathews Volunteer Rescue Squad and are active in their church, Kingston Parrish. They have three grown children and five grandchildren.

TOM PARKER is a senior vice president of Yukon, an Alongside Management Company based in Richmond, Virginia that specializes in customized negotiations training. Tom has more than twenty-five years of sales, marketing, product development, and sales management experience with large multinational corporations.

After earning his MBA at the Darden School of Business at the University of Virginia, Tom joined Rubbermaid Commercial Products. He rose through the sales and marketing organizations and ultimately ran their Office Products Division. Some of the products that Tom developed while at Rubbermaid remain top sellers today.

In late 1987, Tom was recruited by Richmond businessman Bill Goodwin to help rescue AMF Bowling. Tom was brought in to restructure and refocus the sales group. During his ten years as vice president of sales with AMF, Tom was part of a very successful turnaround that led to a $1.3 billion buyout by Goldman Sachs and an IPO.

Over the course of his career, Tom has managed company salesmen, manufacturer's reps, telemarketers, and distributors. He has created compensation systems, business plans, budgets, quotas, sales

contests, and incentive plans. He has negotiated large national contracts and international joint ventures.

In addition to his corporate career, he owned and operated two small service businesses for several years.

Since joining Alongside Management, Tom has conducted negotiation seminars and training sessions throughout the United States as well as in Asia, Europe, Africa, South America, and Australia.

Tom has written articles on negotiation, and he speaks regularly to business and civic groups on the subject. He also coauthored a course on negotiations for women and authored a course on negotiations for Realtors.

He has been active on industry and trade association boards and has consulted for several years with a multinational manufacturer of vending machines.

Tom and his wife, Betsy, live in Richmond, Virginia, and have two grown sons.